INNOVATION
AND
GROWTH

What Do We Know?

INNOVATION AND GROWTH

What Do We Know?

editor

Anjan Thakor

Washington University in St. Louis, USA

World Scientific

NEW JERSEY • LONDON • SINGAPORE • BEIJING • SHANGHAI • HONG KONG • TAIPEI • CHENNAI

Published by

World Scientific Publishing Co. Pte. Ltd.

5 Toh Tuck Link, Singapore 596224

USA office: 27 Warren Street, Suite 401-402, Hackensack, NJ 07601

UK office: 57 Shelton Street, Covent Garden, London WC2H 9HE

British Library Cataloguing-in-Publication Data
A catalogue record for this book is available from the British Library.

INNOVATION AND GROWTH
What Do We Know?

ISBN 978-981-4343-53-4

In-house Editor: Yvonne Tan

Typeset by Stallion Press
Email: enquiries@stallionpress.com

Printed in Singapore

Contents

Chapter 1

Innovation: An Overview

Anjan Thakor

This chapter provides an overview of this book on innovation. The book has two parts. The first part contains chapters that provide reviews of the academic research on innovation. The academic research reviewed includes the research in organizational behavior, operations, marketing, economics and finance. The second part contains chapters that provide a variety of perspectives on innovation for managers that are practically useful and implementable. The authors of the chapters are faculty at the Olin Business School at Washington University in St. Louis. The book is thus unusual in that it brings together a synthesis of academic research on innovation with a variety of cross-functional and very practical managerial perspectives on innovation.

1. Introduction

This is an ambitious book whose purpose is twofold. First, it seeks to provide a synthesis of the academic research on innovation from a multi-functional perspective. A diverse set of functions — organizational behavior, operations, marketing, economics and finance — are covered. The reader should thus be able to gain a good understanding of the large body of academic research on innovation in many different business disciplines. Second, the book seeks to provide practically implementable insights for managers who are interested in improving the innovation capabilities of their organizations. The chapters devoted to this, cover a wide range of issues ranging from organizational culture and changing the mindset of the organization to the specifics of how one should contract for innovation and avoid common myths in innovation.

The book thus melds academic research with down-to-earth, practical insights on how organizations can become more innovative. All the contributing authors are faculty at the Olin Business School at Washington University in St. Louis, USA, with one exception — a consultant (Signe Spencer) with considerable experience in the area. The views expressed in this book thus have strong research support and intellectual depth.

This book is launched under the auspices of the Institute for Innovation and Growth (IIG) and the Wells Fargo Advisors Center for Finance and Accounting Research (WFA-CFAR), new research centers launched by the Olin Business School that are dedicated to innovation and finance and accounting research. The main goals of the IIG and WFA-CFAR are to stimulate research on innovation as well as finance, accounting and organizations, and then disseminate it through publications, consulting projects for organizations, courses, and conferences.

The rest of this chapter is organized as follows. In Section 2, I discuss the first part of the book. In Section 3, I discuss the second part. Section 4 concludes.

2. The Academic Research on Innovation

In the first part of the book, there are three chapters that provide syntheses of the academic research on innovation from many different perspectives. Sawyer and Bunderson (S–B) review the research on organizational behavior. Kouvelis and Lus (K–L) review the academic research on managing the innovation process and the new product development process from operations and marketing research perspectives. Thakor reviews the innovation research in finance.

Organizational Behavior

S–B review studies of organizational innovation that focus on groups and teams. The reason for this is that there is consensus among organization researchers that most of the innovation that occurs in organizations happens in groups and teams. Examples include cross-functional task forces, process improvement committees, new product development teams, and top management groups. The idea is that teams deliver innovative breakthroughs by combining knowledge and cross-functional perspectives from various parts of the organization.

However, just forming cross-functional teams and unleashing them onto the task of innovation is not enough. In order to realize the innovation potential of these teams, they should be structured and managed in ways that increase the opportunity for useful creative ideas to be recognized, selected and then combined effectively to generate innovation. S–B survey the academic research on this and find that the literature falls into four broad categories. These categories are: *team composition, team process, team norms* and *team organizational contexts* that are associated with innovation outcomes.

On the issue of *team composition*, the literature on innovation in groups has focused on *group diversity* and *group turnover.* Regarding *group diversity*, the common perception is that diversity promotes innovation. However, the literature has found that this common perception misses key subtleties. In particular, diversity complicates interpersonal relations and heightens conflicts, thereby possibly offsetting the benefits of breadth of perspective. The key to making diversity a net benefit is to have group members committed to the group and its goals. Regarding *group turnover*, the authors conclude that the empirical evidence is unclear and ambiguous. There is, however, some emerging evidence that turnover is more likely to promote innovation in firms with complex, knowledge-intensive, problem-driven tasks than in firms that have routine, coordination-intensive, process-driven tasks.

On the issue of *team process*, the authors provide a very thorough survey. One of their surprising findings is that despite the increasing popularity of brainstorming as a technique to spur innovation, there is substantial research evidence that brainstorming groups are less effective at generating ideas than the same number of people working alone in a "virtual" group. They go on to identify factors that make brainstorming more or less effective.

On the issue of *team norms*, the authors review numerous factors that are associated with stronger versus weaker learning norms in teams. They discuss three factors that have emerged as the most significant: psychological safety, power asymmetry and openness to diversity.

Finally, the authors point out that teams never operate in a vacuum — each team is a part of a broader *organizational context*. They go on to discuss a variety of ways in which organizational context affects innovation. They also discuss at length the significant strides made in recent decades by researchers on assessing and evaluating the informal organization through the use of social network analysis. The role of creativity is also examined.

At the end of their chapter, S–B discuss how the framework emerging from their literature review can be put into practice. They make the following key points:

(1)   Social ties can help people be more creative, can help teams be more creative and can help organizations be more innovative. The research reviewed by S–B identifies several characteristics of social networks that are associated with enhanced creativity.

(2)   At the individual level, it is best to be connected but not too connected. It is best to have some number of weak ties, in addition to the strong ties that characterize most work teams and organizational units. Individuals should also seek out ties outside of their local, dense network.

(3)   At the team level, although team cohesion is associated with greater work satisfaction and efficiency, it runs the risk of reducing team creativity. Team members should make sure to remain connected outside of their team. Team leaders should:

   •   provide incentives to members who bring information from external ties;
   •   give time in the schedule for these ties to be pursued;
   •   watch out for too much cohesiveness.

(4)   At the organization level, a small world structure is more innovative than either a network with all dense ties, or a network with exclusively weak ties. Organization leaders can increase the likelihood of a small world structure by:

   •   frequent reassignment of staff;
   •   innovation labs;
   •   shadowing staff in another unit;
   •   incentive systems that reward cross-unit contacts and exchange of information;
   •   office space architecture that increases the likelihood of encounters with different others that might lead to a weak tie being formed.

Operations and Marketing

In this chapter, K–L review the academic research in operations and marketing to provide insights into how the innovation process, particularly new product development projects, should be managed. They begin by noting the importance of new product development to firms — almost 30% of companies' sales are from new products.

Because the literature on the subject is vast, the review focuses on a few selected topics such as Platform-Based Product Development, Disruptive Innovation, Portfolio Management and Resource Allocation, and Incentives.

On the issue of *Platform-Based Product Development*, the authors note that it provides several important benefits to companies in industrial practice, including the greater flexibility of tailoring products to meet the varying needs of different customer segments, reduction in system complexity, shorter product lead-times, reduction in unit production costs, and improved service levels and competitiveness within the marketplace. There are many examples in practice. One of the most successful stories of product development using the platform-based approach is by Kodak in the development of its single-use cameras. This case study is discussed in depth in the chapter.

Next, the authors discuss *Disruptive Innovation*, which is one of the most important innovations that threatens the competitiveness and survival of many top companies in their industries. The concept of disruptive innovation was first introduced by Clayton Christensen with the concept of sustaining innovation. Sustaining innovation can be described as an incremental (or radical) increase in the performance and features of an existing product in an established market. Such innovation initially targets the high-end of the existing market to derive the best customers' higher margins, and then spreads downward through the low-end market segment over time. An example of a sustaining innovation is the evolution of Pentium processors with new features added in every model which attract the high-end customers at first.

Disruptive innovation, by contrast, brings a new product into the market which initially underperforms the existing product in the key dimensions that the high-end customers value, but is more appealing to low-end market or new customers on alternate dimensions such as its lower price, simplicity and more convenience of use.

The research question is: what is the impact of disruptive innovation on existing and emerging markets, and when does it pay for a firm to engage in disruptive innovation? The authors' research indicates that the answer depends on whether the innovation is offered to the market by the incumbent firm or by a new entrant, the difference between the maximum price the customer is willing to pay and the manufacturer's unit production cost, and the relative appeal of the product (whether broad or niche). The authors conclude by observing that more research is needed on *how to position* new products in the market.

On the issue of *Portfolio Management and Resource Allocation*, the authors focus on the literature that has examined project selection processes and resource allocation processes. The question is: how do you optimally manage project portfolios, so that both routine and innovative projects receive the necessary resources? Unless this is done, innovative ideas may die due to lack of organizational resources.

Their survey of the literature reveals that different types of projects require *different management processes*. While radical breakthrough projects face higher risks and uncertainties, the ones associated with incremental/derivative projects are lower. It is clear that firms should invest in the development of both breakthrough projects and incremental projects in order to remain competitive in the market. The incremental projects may require very tightly controlled processes. Breakthrough innovations require processes that are much more tolerant of risk and accommodate longer payback periods.

Finally, on the issue of *Incentives*, the authors note that to reduce the cycle time for introducing new products, companies need to focus on the impact of funding authority and incentives on the dynamic allocation of resources between different innovative projects over a specified portfolio review cycle. The research suggests that managers have higher incentives for their efforts when they are given funding authority. However, giving authority to the managers who make the resource allocation decisions as well as their increased career concerns shift the balance of the project portfolio towards a more incremental strategy, i.e., the manager's interest is in investing in improvements to existing products. While this provides higher profits in the short run, it will affect the firms' long-run success and competitiveness in a negative way. One possible future research direction is to develop proper incentive schemes that increase the managers' willingness to allocate more resources to radical breakthrough projects, thereby shifting the portfolio balance towards a radical strategy.

Finance and Economics

My chapter on the role of innovation in Finance and Economics reviews two strands of literature on innovation in Finance and Economics. The first has to do with how innovation is financed and its impact on shareholder value. The second has to do with *financial innovation*, which is the process by which new financial securities and structures are created. In both cases, I discuss the managerial decision-making implications.

On the first strand, I address four questions. The first is: does innovation create shareholder value? What is the evidence? The research on this indicates that it does, but the impact is industry-specific. Moreover, the answer to the question depends on what kind of value we are talking about. It appears that *on average,* entrepreneurs are inadequately rewarded for the risk they take in innovative ventures. However, entrepreneurs engage in such activity because they are optimistic, and this produces benefits for society. That is, "social value" is created from innovation, even though entrepreneurs earn inadequate risk-adjusted returns on average.

The second question is: why do firms do basic research that does not directly generate a product with revenue potential? The research on this reveals that most people think of the research that firms wish to engage in as "applied research", which is research that can be converted into commercially profitable products and services. However, firms also engage in basic or fundamental research, even though there is high uncertainty and it is difficult for the firm investing in that research to appropriate all the rents. The question is why. My review chapter lists a variety of factors that induce firms to engage in basic research, including the important point that basic research by firms is often done *accidentally* while they are in the pursuit of applied research. These factors also provide guidance to managers about when basic research makes sense.

The third question is: how do companies set hurdle rates for innovative projects? Here the research indicates that the correct approach is to view innovative projects as real options, and there are quantitative techniques for valuing these options.

The fourth question is: how do innovative firms get financed? In response to this, the chapter reviews a large body of work on venture capital and initial public offerings (IPOs), as well as some research on how compensation contracts should be written to incentivize managers to engage in innovative projects.

The second strand of the literature being reviewed has to do with financial innovation. Again, four questions are studied. The first is: how do we define financial innovation? The literature survey shows that the definition includes not only new instruments, but also new technologies, institutions, and markets. The number of financial innovations introduced in the past 30 years that satisfy this definition is enormous.

The second question is: why is there so much financial innovation? Here the literature review reveals half a dozen factors that generate innovation incentives, including technological shocks, globalization, taxes and regulation. These factors are discussed in depth in the chapter.

The third question is: who are the innovators and what are their incentives? Here the literature indicates that the innovators are financial institutions, especially investment banks, and that innovation incentives are stronger in functionally-separated financial systems — like the one in the US when the Glass–Steagall Act separation of commercial banking from investment banking and insurance was in place — than in universal banking systems. Morever, large firms and those affected most adversely by existing market conditions innovate the most.

The final question covered in the chapter is: what are the social benefits of innovation? Although there is no consensus on this, it appears that financial innovations can benefit society by improving market liquidity and lowering the cost of capital for firms.

Thus, my review chapter reveals numerous insights that have emerged from the academic research on the financing of innovations in non-financial firms and the process of financial innovation that is dominated by financial firms.

3. Innovation Insights from a Managerial Perspective

In the second part of the book, there are four chapters that provide a wealth of new innovation insights for managers. In the first chapter, Konczak and Spencer ask how business leaders can update the right climate for innovation within their organizations. They note that "organizational climate" refers to employees' perceptions of how it feels to work in a particular setting. These perceptions affect employees' performance. They identify six dimensions of organizational climate that affect employees' ability to perform. Emerging from their discussion is a very interesting framework that leaders can use to align their organizations with the optimal innovation output from their employees.

In the second chapter in this part of the book, Chun and Thakor describe an approach to innovation that can be used by individuals as well as organizations. They call it the "unblocking" approach. The idea is that the ability to innovate is impeded by the *assumptions* we make about the situation we are in. These assumptions define the *paradigm* we operate within, and they may be explicit or implicit. Because we choose to operate mostly within the box defined by our assumptions, we fail to see the possibilities that lie outside the box. Recognizing these possibilities requires identifying and discarding an important assumption about our paradigm, and this is not easy to do because each assumption often has ample empirical support. For example, airlines operate under the assumption that the only thing customers care about is price and that the main component of price they will focus on is the most *salient* — the basic ticket price without any of the add-ons for extra bags, extra leg room, etc. The authors identify a systematic approach that can be used to determine which assumptions of the paradigm should be challenged in order to pursue innovation. They discuss numerous case studies and outline practically implementable steps.

In the next chapter entitled "Contracting for Innovation", Argyres examines how organizations should manage relationships with parties outside the organization who come up with innovative ideas. He discusses three approaches to managing these relationships: contract design, relational governance, and tournaments. He also examines the relative importance of the three approaches. He concludes that contract design is perhaps the most generally applicable approach and thus deserves special attention from managers. He identifies settings in which relational governance or tournaments may be important mechanisms as well.

Finally, Knott's chapter examines numerous myths about innovation in general and about R&D in particular. She identifies some of the findings that have emerged from past research that seem to have intuitive appeal. She then focuses on more recent research that combines insider experience with more sophisticated data and methods, and argues that many of the prescriptions from past theory are invalid. For example, she points out that a widely-held belief appears to be that spillovers and imitation by others dilute the innovation incentives of firms. However, the research she reviews shows that innovation is highest in industries with the highest spillover rates. This has the striking implication — counter to conventional wisdom — that patents probably have only minimal impact on innovation.

Collectively, these four chapters point out that there is a wealth of practically relevant research on innovation from which managers can learn. Many widely-held beliefs about innovation are wrong. Stimulating innovation is not just an art — it is a science too.

4. Conclusion

This is a book on innovation that has taken the unusual approach of surveying the academic research on innovation from many different functional perspectives, and has also included various chapters that address specific decision-making issues in innovation for managers. A plethora of insights are contained in these chapters. A distinguishing feature of these insights is that they are based on research, and they also explore a variety of myths about what innovation is and how it should be nurtured.

Part A:

The Academic Research on Innovation

Chapter 2

Innovation: A Review of Research in Organizational Behavior

Keith Sawyer

Washington University in St. Louis

Stuart Bunderson

Olin Business School,
Washington University in St. Louis

There is a consensus among organization researchers that most of the innovation that takes place in organizations happens in groups and teams. This chapter reviews studies of organizational innovation that focus on groups and teams. Examples include cross-functional task forces, process improvement committees, new product development teams, and top management groups. Teams hold the promise of delivering real innovative breakthroughs by combining knowledge and perspective from different parts of an organization in order to generate new ways of thinking about products, processes, or markets. But in order to realize this innovative potential, teams must be structured and managed in ways that increase the opportunity for useful creative ideas to be recognized, selected, and then combined with other creative ideas to generate organizational innovation. Our chapter groups this literature into four broad categories: team composition, team process, team norms, and team organizational contexts that are associated with innovation outcomes.

Organizational innovation can be studied at several different levels of analysis. One might choose to focus on the most basic element of an organization, the individual, and study the mental processes associated with new ideas. At the other extreme, one might choose to focus on the organization as a whole — its culture, structure, and processes — or even on the organization's external environment. In this review, we focus on a critical mediating level of analysis, the group. Groups are critical to organizational innovation, because they are where individual creative ideas are combined to generate organizational innovation (Sawyer, 2007). Scholars in organizational behavior study several aspects of groups that are causally related to innovation outcomes: team composition, diversity, organizational climate and culture, leadership, incentives and motivation, and many others.

However, no exhaustive overview of this research has been published to date. This gap is perhaps more surprising given that so many recent literature reviews have focused on groups and teams in organizations (e.g., Kozlowski and Bell, 2003; Kozlowski and Ilgen, 2006; Mannix and Neale, 2005). These reviews focus on team effectiveness and team processes in general; although some of these findings may have implications for innovation in teams, these reviews do not identify or elaborate those implications.

A second group of recent literature reviews has focused on the individual psychological processes associated with creativity (George, 2007; Runco, 2004; Shalley, Zhou, and Oldham, 2004; Zhou and Shalley, 2003). These studies also have implications for innovation in organizations. However, most scholars of innovation agree that individual creativity has a problematic relation with organizational innovation. Consequently, these psychological reviews are of only limited usefulness to scholars studying organizational innovation.

We define innovation as a useful and appropriate organization-level outcome — in contrast to creativity, which we define as an idea that originates with an individual. In our conception, creativity research is the realm of psychology, whereas innovation research is the realm of organizational behavior. Studies of the history of innovation have revealed that organizational innovations almost always are combinations of many individual ideas — in some cases, even hundreds of ideas (think of the many creative decisions that contribute to a single Hollywood movie, a modern videogame, or a software application such as Microsoft Word).

Our review centers on innovation in groups. There is a consensus across organization researchers that most of the innovation that takes place in organizations happens within the context of groups and teams. Examples include cross-functional task forces, process improvement committees, new product development teams, and top management groups. Teams hold the promise of delivering real innovative breakthroughs by combining knowledge and perspective from different parts of an organization in order to generate new ways of thinking about products, processes, or markets. But in order to realize this innovative potential, teams must be structured and managed in ways that increase the opportunity for useful creative ideas to be recognized, selected, and then combined with other creative ideas to generate organizational innovation.

Based on our current understandings of the literature, we have observed that this literature can be organized into four broad categories: team composition, team process, team norms, and team organizational contexts that are associated with innovation outcomes.

1. Composition

While it may be true that a group cannot be described solely as the sum of its individual parts (i.e., members), it is also true that the various parts that make up a group, and their individual and collective characteristics, have a significant bearing on the way a group functions. We therefore begin our discussion of innovation in groups with a consideration of the way that group composition affects innovative efforts and innovative outcomes in groups. Specifically, we will consider two key elements of group composition that have received attention in the literature on innovation in groups: group diversity and group turnover.

Group Diversity

In 1848, the philosopher John Stuart Mill made the following observation: "It is hardly possible to overrate the value ... of placing human beings in contact with persons dissimilar to themselves, and with modes of thought and action unlike those with which they are familiar. [...] Such communication has always been, and is particularly in the present age, one of the primary sources of progress." This quotation captures a key premise underlying investigations of the relationship between diversity and innovation, namely, that we would expect to see more frequent and more significant innovations in social settings that place people "in contact with persons dissimilar to themselves" since those settings make possible the novel combination of different "modes of thought and action" (see Kanter, 1988). It follows that we should see more innovation in groups that are diverse in ways that lead to real differences in these "modes of thought and action" among group members. So, for example, we might expect to find greater innovation in groups with diverse membership in terms of age, gender, tenure, education, functional background, divisional affiliation, etc. (see Milliken and Martins, 1996; Tsui *et al.*, 1995).

The research provides some evidence to support this assertion. For example, Bantel and Jackson (1989) found that diversity in the functional backgrounds of members of top management teams in the banking industry was associated with more organizational innovation and, particularly, innovations in administrative processes. Similarly, Hambrick, Cho, and Chen (1996) found that the diversity of top management teams in the air-line industry in terms of functional background and education was associated with competitive moves that were seen as bolder and more innovative by industry observers. Keck (1997) studied firms in the cement and computer industries and found that those firms that adapted to turbulence in the business environment had top management teams who were more diverse in their functional affiliations. In two related studies, Lant, Milliken, and Batra (1992) and Wiersema and Bantel (1992) found that management teams were more likely to pursue novel strategic directions when they were diverse in terms of functional affiliation or educational background. And the literature on minority influence (e.g., Nemeth, 1986) suggests that the presence of even one group member who disagrees with the majority can deepen cognitive processing and lead to more reflective and integrative outcomes. In short, the empirical evidence appears to support a positive relationship between group diversity and innovative actions and results.

The research evidence also clearly suggests, however, that diversity in groups can complicate interpersonal relations and heighten intra-group conflict and that these "process losses" have the potential to offset any advantages gained through a breadth of perspective within a group. The very differences in background and perspective that generate novel insights can also create communication difficulties and lead to disagreement about how to interpret or prioritize information. Moreover, member differences in background are also often correlated with fundamental ideological differences that make integration and compromise difficult if not impossible. In short, team diversity has a darker side. In a study of 76 top management teams, Knight *et al.* (1999) found, for example, that teams with a greater diversity of member functional backgrounds experienced higher interpersonal conflict and had more difficulty achieving consensus. Studies by Pelled, Eisenhardt, and Xin (1999) and Jehn, Northcraft, and Neale (1999) also suggested that higher intra-group diversity leads to higher levels of intra-group conflict. This documented tendency for diversity to promote conflict is often cited as the most likely explanation in studies that fail to find a relationship between group diversity and innovation or that find a negative relationship (e.g., Ancona and Caldwell, 1992).

How, then, can we predict whether diversity in member knowledge and expertise will lead to the productive interchange of different ideas that fosters innovation, or to destructive conflicts and interpersonal tensions that breed suspicion and stalemate? Research by Van der Vegt and Bunderson (2005) points to one key factor — the degree to which group members are committed to the group and its goals. In a study of 57 interdisciplinary research teams in a global oil and gas company, they found that diversity in disciplinary affiliation was positively associated with more innovative team behavior in teams where members identified with and felt emotionally attached to their team, and negatively associated with innovative behavior in teams where members lacked that sense of emotional attachment. They point out that because diversity in groups is associated with member differences in perspective and priority, integrating those differences in order to gain new insights is interpersonally risky and takes real effort. And group members are simply less likely to invest that effort if they do not identify with and feel emotionally invested in the group, its members, and its goals. Where members lack that investment, diversity is likely to pull the group apart before any meaningful insights are gained. The authors suggest that this sense of commitment and identification can be fostered in a group by creating a situation in which member actions and/or outcomes are interdependent, e.g., through the creation of group-based goals and incentives or the establishment of task interdependencies.

The study by Van der Vegt and Bunderson (2005) raises another important question about the relationship between team diversity and innovative behavior in teams. Specifically, they find that it is possible for teams to have too much diversity. When team members are too different in terms of their backgrounds and worldviews, there is little common ground on which to build in leveraging those differences or converging on promising syntheses. As a result, groups in which members have little in common may find it difficult to realize the benefits of diversity regardless of how committed members are to the team and its goals. Put differently, the relationship between team diversity and innovative behavior in teams may actually resemble an inverted U, i.e., the relationship is positive at lower-to-moderate levels of team diversity but becomes negative at high and very high levels of diversity. This is precisely the relationship that Van der Vegt and Bunderson (2005) found for the high-commitment teams in their study.

Group Turnover

Another, more dynamic, element of group composition with relevance for a group's innovative behavior and outcomes is the rate and magnitude of member turnover within the group. Turnover involves the entry of new members into a group and/or the exit of existing members from the group (Levine, Choi, and Moreland, 2003). Given that member turnover can affect a broad range of group processes and outcomes, turnover has received a good deal of attention in the small groups literature (Arrow and McGrath, 1995; Dalton, 1997; Shaw *et al.*, 2005). Our purpose here is to briefly review studies that have specifically examined the effect of turnover on innovative behavior and/or innovative outcomes in groups. Perhaps not surprisingly, given the pervasive implications of member turnover for groups, our review will suggest that turnover has important implications for innovation in groups, but that those implications are more complex and nuanced than we might think.

On one hand, turnover could promote innovation because the entry of new members or the departure of existing members could serve to disrupt the habitual and often mindless patterns of thought and interaction that have been shown to emerge in stable groups (Katz, 1982). When turnover occurs, groups may be forced to rethink member roles, revisit task routines, articulate long-standing norms to new members, and restructure internal coalitions. All of these activities present opportunities for the group to identify and pursue innovative improvements to existing practice.

In other words, group turnover can be a powerful trigger for innovation in groups.

There is some evidence to suggest that this is, in fact, the case. Ziller, Behringer, and Goodchilds (1962) found, for example, that laboratory groups which either added or lost a member generated more new ideas than stable groups. In a related study, Arrow and McGrath (1993) found that laboratory groups with an experimentally imposed new member and groups with member absences performed better on a task requiring reflection about the group's internal process. Virany, Tushman, and Romanelli (1992) found that change in a CEO and/or other members of a top management team can enable more adaptive responses to changes in a business environment. And several studies have documented the tendency for newcomers to introduce new practices and insights into the groups that they join, although the evidence also suggests that the ability of a newcomer to promote innovation is contingent on characteristics of both the newcomer and the group (Choi and Levine, 2004; Gruenfeld, Martorana, and Fan, 2000; Kane, Argote, and Levine, 2005).

On the other hand, there is also evidence to suggest that turnover does not inevitably promote either innovative behavior or innovative outcomes. While it may be true that turnover can encourage (or even force) innovation and can provide the raw materials for that innovation in the form of new ideas and new relationships, it is also the case that turnover can introduce an element of uncertainty or even mistrust into a group since members do not know one another. And past research has strongly suggested that a climate of uncertainty and mistrust can severely dampen the willingness of group members to engage in innovative, learning-oriented behaviors (Edmondson, 1999). Innovation and learning are more likely to emerge in teams where there is a climate of "psychological safety", a climate that is fostered under conditions of group stability where members can get to know one another and develop norms of openness and trust (Moreland and Levine, 2002; O'Connor, Gruenfeld, and McGrath, 1993). Consistent with this more cautious view of the effects of turnover on innovation, Argote *et al.* (1995) found that laboratory groups without any member turnover had steeper learning curves than groups that experienced turnover, even when tasks were complex. And Van der Vegt, Bunderson, and Kuipers (2009) found that turnover in a sample of self-managed production teams was negatively associated with innovative (learning-oriented) behavior as measured by the team. They also found no evidence for a curvilinear relationship between turnover and innovative behavior; the relationship was negative and monotonic.

As with team diversity, we find ourselves facing an unclear and ambiguous pattern of empirical findings. Some research suggests that member turnover can provide a prime opportunity for innovation within groups, while other research shows that turnover does not always do so. The key challenge for researchers, then, is to identify those factors that allow groups to take advantage of the "innovation opportunity" presented by member turnover. Some progress has been made in the identification of those factors. We know, for example, that turnover is more likely to promote innovation (i.e., "useful and appropriate" actions per our earlier definition) in dynamic or rapidly changing environments where protecting and refining task routines is less important than updating those routines in response to task demands (Keck, 1997; Virany, Tushman, and Romanelli, 1992). There is also some emerging evidence to suggest that turnover is more likely to promote innovation for complex, knowledge-intensive, problem-driven tasks (e.g., consulting) than for routine, coordination-intensive, process-driven tasks (e.g., production or manufacturing) (e.g., Argote *et al.*, 1995).

2. Process

Teams generate innovation through interaction among members of the team. If the interactions are predictable and scripted, or if they are too strongly controlled by the team leader or by the strict norms and procedures of the organization, then no unexpected innovations will emerge. Teams are more likely to generate innovation when the group processes are emergent, unpredictable, and improvisational (Sawyer, 2007). Yet, research also shows that completely unstructured team interactions are not the ideal; the introduction of an appropriate structure to guide the team's creative process can enhance the innovation potential of the team.

Perhaps the most widely used technique for guiding and enhancing a group's creative process is *brainstorming*. Brainstorming was developed by advertising executive Alex Osborn, of BBDO, in the 1940s and 1950s, and was described in his 1953 book *Applied Imagination* (Osborn, 1953). Brainstorming is based on two principles that Osborn called "deferment of judgment" and "quantity breeds quality." *Deferment of judgment* means that idea generation should be strictly separated from idea evaluation. From these two principles, Osborn proposed the following four guidelines for a brainstorming session. First, no criticism; do not evaluate any of the ideas, brainstorming is for idea generation, and evaluation is to come later. Second, "freewheeling" is encouraged; the wilder the idea, the better. Third, quantity is the goal; the more ideas presented, the more likely that more creative ideas will be among them. Fourth, everyone should look for combinations of previous ideas, and improvements on previous ideas. Osborn claimed that following these rules would more than double the ideas generated by group members.

Some of today's most innovative companies are strong advocates of brainstorming. Perhaps the best known is IDEO, a product design firm based in Silicon Valley (Kelley, 2001; Sutton and Hargadon, 1996). Each designer at IDEO spends five to ten percent of his or her time engaged in brainstorming sessions. IDEO has added a few additional rules to the four originally proposed by Osborn, such as "stay focused on the topic," "stick to one conversation at a time," and "be physical and use the space." In addition, their sessions are always led by a trained facilitator.

In spite of the continued popularity of brainstorming as a technique, there is a substantial body of research literature documenting that brainstorming groups are less effective at generating ideas than the same number of people, working alone, who later pool their ideas — what has become known as a *nominal group* (because the individuals are working alone, they are a group in name only). The productivity score of a nominal group is based on the quantity and quality of the non-redundant ideas of n individuals working alone, where n is the number of people working together in the brainstorming group. "Non-redundant" means that if an idea is suggested several times by different individuals, the duplicates are eliminated so that the nominal group only gets credit for one instance of the idea (because in real groups, it would be inappropriate for members to suggest the same idea several times). The productivity and quality of ideas produced by these nominal groups of individuals working alone is a baseline representing the creativity of individuals who are not helped nor inhibited by group interaction.

In addition to the quantity of ideas, several studies have measured the quality of ideas generated. After all, a lot of ideas is not helpful if the quality is low. Studies have used several different measures of quality of an idea, such as originality (measured by how infrequently the idea is suggested) or feasibility (measured by ratings of independent evaluators). Most studies that analyze quality use a measure of total quality, summing up the quality ratings of all of the ideas generated. Because total quality is highly related to the total number of ideas generated, some researchers prefer to use the average quality of an idea, by dividing total quality by the total number of ideas. Other researchers argue that the total number of good ideas — ideas that receive a score above a chosen threshold — is the best measure of a group's creativity.

The first study that found that brainstorming actually inhibits creativity was published in 1958 (Taylor, Berry, and Block, 1958). Taylor *et al.* asked subjects to brainstorm for 12 minutes, either individually or in four-person groups. Nominal groups were formed from the subjects who had brainstormed individually; for each nominal group, the ideas generated by four individuals were combined, eliminating redundant ideas. Taylor *et al.* found that the nominal groups generated twice as many different ideas as the real groups. In recent years, multiple studies have found that brainstorming groups, on average, generate half as many ideas as a similar number of solitary individuals, and the group does not generate higher quality ideas, either (as reviewed in Diehl and Stroebe, 1987; Stroebe and Diehl, 1994). Diehl and Stroebe (1987) listed 22 experiments, and found that in 18 of them, the nominal groups outperformed the real groups; in only four — all involving two-person groups — there was no difference. In one meta-analytic review of these studies, Mullen, Johnson, and Salas (1991) concluded that both quantity and quality of ideas is lower in brainstorming groups than in the comparison nominal groups. Quantity of ideas and number of good ideas are typically highly correlated; Diehl and Stroebe (1987, 1991) found a correlation of .80 between quantity of ideas and number of good ideas.

Factors that Make Brainstorming More or Less Effective

Thus, by the mid-1980s, there was a strong consensus among creativity researchers that brainstorming groups were less creative than nominal groups, a phenomenon that became known as *productivity loss* — referring to the lost productivity of groups compared to solo individuals. This resulted in a second phase of brainstorming research: the attempt to discover the factors that caused this productivity loss, in the hopes of understanding how to design groups to be more creative. In an influential early study of productivity loss in groups, Steiner (1972) distinguished two forms of productivity loss: *motivation losses* and *co-ordination losses*. Motivation losses might occur if something about the group situation lowers the motivation of group members below that of subjects that work alone; Steiner identified two motivation losses: *free riding* and *production matching*. Co-ordination losses result from the difficulties in co-ordinating individual contributions to the group product; Steiner identified two co-ordination losses: *evaluation apprehension* and *production blocking*.

Motivation losses

Free riding refers to a classic phenomenon studied by social psychologists: that individuals in a group might "free ride" on the efforts of others. For example, in a group of six individuals, one of the individuals might reason that if he were to stay quiet and relax a bit, the other five members would generate plenty of ideas and no one would ever notice his silence. Several brainstorming researchers have attributed productivity loss to free riding (e.g., Stroebe and Frey, 1982). This could occur for two reasons: first, everyone knows that their ideas will be summed at the end of the session, so they might feel that their individual contribution is less identifiable. Second, group members might reason that their contribution is less important, and thus more dispensable.

The free-rider interpretation accounts for several findings from brainstorming research. Bouchard (1972) introduced a rule that participants had to give their ideas in a predetermined sequence, and if they could not think of a new idea, they had to say "pass." Bouchard found that this rule increased group productivity, suggesting that making contributions identifiable reduces free riding. Bouchard and Hare (1970) examined groups of sizes 5, 7, and 9, and found that the larger the group, the bigger the productivity loss for the interactive group. The free riding hypothesis would predict that increases in group size would increase dispensability and decrease identifiability, thus explaining the increase in productivity loss with larger groups.

If the group is told that quantity is the only measure of their performance, then the task becomes additive, and every single contribution would be important. If the group is told that quality or originality is the goal, then group members that think they are less creative might think their ideas are more dispensable (Kerr and Bruun, 1983).

Production matching refers to a phenomenon where individuals compare their own performance to that of the other group members, and they try to match their level of production to that of the others. It is well-known that setting ambitious goals can increase performance, including with idea generation (e.g., Hyams and Graham, 1984). Paulus and Dzindolet (1993) reasoned that because brainstorming is a new situation for most people, they are not sure about what would be the appropriate level of productivity. Consequently, they will reduce their uncertainty by comparing their performance to that of others in the group. If this hypothesis is correct, then there should be a convergence of individual productivity towards the mean — rather than the observed lower performance of interactive versus nominal groups. In an experimental comparison of interactive and nominal brainstorming groups, Paulus and Dzindolet (1993) found that the number of ideas generated by individuals was more highly correlated in the interactive groups than in the nominal groups, providing support to the production matching hypothesis. Paulus and Dzindolet explained the lower productivity of interactive groups by making two additional assumptions: first, in the early phases of the brainstorming session, individual productivity is inhibited due to co-ordination losses (see below); then, due to production matching, the low performance becomes a group norm and keeps productivity down. However, the evidence for this was inconclusive. They found that there was less decrease in productivity, over the 25-minute session, for interacting groups than for nominal groups; however, even in the interacting groups, there was a decrease in productivity — on average, in the first five minutes, the interacting groups generated 12.9 ideas, and in the final five minutes, generated only 5.5 ideas. This seems inconsistent with the hypothesis that the group establishes a low norm at the beginning which then remains constant through the entire session.

Co-ordination losses

Evaluation apprehension or *social inhibition* suggests that group members are monitoring the quality of their own ideas, and resist voicing all of the ideas that occur to them — contrary to the brainstorming instructions to "freewheel" and not worry about criticism. This would occur in a group setting because individuals are afraid of negative evaluations from other group members; however, in the solitary nominal condition, those who will be reviewing the ideas generated are not physically present, reducing the potential risk of negative evaluation. Early support for social inhibition came from a study by Collaros and Anderson (1969) who manipulated the perceived expertise of group members in the brainstorming group. The logic behind the experiment was that each individual would be more inhibited if they thought the other members were experts. The experiment had three conditions: all experts, when each member of the group was told that all other members had previous experience with such groups; one expert, when each member of the group was told that only one unidentified member of the group had previously worked in such a group; and no experts, when no such instructions were provided. The results were consistent with the predictions: productivity was highest in the "no experts" condition, and lowest in the "all experts" condition. In a post-experiment questionnaire, the subjects reported more feelings of inhibition in the "all experts" condition.

However, a 1980 study by Maginn and Harris generated inconsistent findings. Their study examined only subjects working alone to generate ideas. Half of the subjects were told that there were three judges on the other side of a one-way mirror who were listening to their ideas and rating them for originality. These subjects generated just as many ideas as the subjects who did not think there were observers, thus finding no evidence for social inhibition. As Stroebe and Diehl (1994) point out, this discrepancy can be explained with a free-rider explanation.

Diehl and Stroebe (1987) further examined this hypothesis by comparing individual (solo) brainstorming on controversial topics with uncontroversial topics. For their controversial topic with German subjects, an example question was: "How can the number of guest workers be reduced?" This is quite controversial politically in Germany, where the study was conducted. Positions on the issue are highly polarized; policies designed to encourage guest workers to return to their home countries are associated with right-wing attitudes, for example. Diehl and Stroebe (1987) further manipulated evaluation apprehension by telling some subjects that their ideas would be evaluated by others. They found that subjects generated fewer ideas with controversial topics, and fewer ideas when they were told their ideas would be evaluated.

Production blocking refers to any aspect of a group's dynamic that results in a reduction in the number of ideas generated. There are several factors that could result in production blocking. First, in a group setting, only one person can talk at a time, whereas the nominal group members, working alone, can all generate ideas in parallel, as it were. Second, if a person cannot voice an idea right when it occurs to them, they might forget the idea before they get a chance to speak; or, they might suppress the idea if they think of a criticism or a reason why it might not work. If, on the other hand, a person manages to keep that idea in mind until the others have finished speaking, this prevents them of thinking of additional ideas during that time. Third, group members have to listen closely to other people's ideas, and this leaves them with less mental energy to generate their own ideas. Research shows that productivity loss increases as the size of the group increases (Bouchard and Hare, 1970).

Diehl and Stroebe (1987) conducted an experiment that demonstrated that production blocking was a major cause of productivity loss in brainstorming groups. They built special communication devices to introduce blocking into the nominal group condition. Each of the four subjects were instructed to speak their ideas into a microphone. Each subject worked alone in a separate room, but all four microphones were connected through a sort of switchboard that acted like a traffic light — allowing only one person to talk at a time. Underneath each microphone was a display of four lights, one corresponding to each group member. Whenever one person was talking, the subject's own light turned green, and the other three turned red. When a person stopped talking for 1.5 seconds, his or her light was switched off, and another person could talk. To further compare the potential role played by social inhibition, Diehl and Stroebe created one condition in which the subjects wore headphones, allowing them to hear the contributions of the others; and a second condition where the subjects did not wear headphones, and could not hear each others' ideas.

The results suggested that production blocking explained almost all of the productivity loss. Nominal groups generated about 100 ideas and face-to-face brainstorming generated about 55 ideas, consistent with prior studies. In the condition where subjects could hear each other, groups generated about 35 ideas; in the condition where they could not, they generated about 40 ideas. Although the hearing condition, which might be expected to introduce social inhibition, resulted in somewhat fewer ideas, the difference was not statistically significant, suggesting that social inhibition does not result in a statistically significant increase in productivity loss, beyond what is explained by production blocking. Furthermore, it suggests that the need to listen to others, thus splitting cognitive capacity between listening and idea generation, is not the cause of production blocking. The cause of productivity loss seems to be the reduction in speaking time available to individuals when brainstorming, compared to solitary individuals in a nominal group.

To further evaluate this hypothesis, Stroebe and Diehl (1994) compared four-person nominal groups given five minutes to generate ideas, with four-person interacting groups given twenty minutes. This condition would allow each individual in the interacting condition to have the same amount of speaking time available as the solo individuals in the nominal group. Stroebe and Diehl found that the interacting groups generated significantly more ideas than the nominal groups — on average, 60.75 ideas versus 47.50 ideas. This might suggest that interacting groups can be more productive; however, these groups not only had four times as much time to talk, they also had four times as much time to think.

To determine whether productivity loss is caused by limiting speaking time or by limited thinking time, Diehl and Stroebe (1991) conducted a variation on the above experiment. They again gave the brainstorming group twenty minutes, but also gave the solo individuals in the nominal condition twenty minutes. However, the solo individuals were only allowed to speak their ideas for a total of five minutes; this was measured with a voice-controlled clock, and the individuals were not allowed to speak any more ideas after their five minutes were up. The results were quite interesting — nominal groups whose individuals could only speak

5 of 20 minutes were almost as productive as nominal groups whose individuals were allowed to talk for the entire 20 minutes; and, their productivity was significantly higher than the interacting group that had 20 minutes.

In this experiment, the solo individuals in the nominal group, and the interacting individuals in the brainstorming group, each had five minutes to talk. The only difference was that the solo individuals could talk whenever they wanted, whereas those in the interacting group had to wait until someone else was finished talking. This study suggests that the waiting time is responsible for productivity loss in brainstorming groups.

A fourth cause of production blocking is *topic fixation*. On any typical brainstorming problem, the ideas generated tend to fall into categories. For example, a common question used on brainstorming experiments with college students — "think of ways to improve your university" — results in ideas that cluster in categories such as improving parking, improving the dining options, improving instruction or classrooms, etc. Ideally, a brainstorming session should generate ideas from as many distinct categories as possible; however, social tendencies in face-to-face groups might limit the range of idea categories considered. First of all, a range of studies has shown that groups tend to talk about information that everyone shares, and tend not to talk about information held only by one individual (e.g., Stasser and Titus, 1985). Second, groups seem to display a tendency toward early consensus, leading to a convergent group style rather than a divergent group style (Aldag and Fuller, 1993).

Larey and Paulus (1999) evaluated the topic fixation hypothesis by developing a measure of *flexibility*, i.e., the total number of categories generated by a group. They had four-person nominal and interactive groups spend 15 minutes generating ideas for "How to improve the campus"; each idea generated was assigned to a category by the researchers. As with prior studies, nominal groups generated almost twice as many ideas (56 versus 31). Nominal groups generated ideas in significantly more categories (17.2 versus 12.1). In a further measure of the topic fixation hypothesis, the researchers analyzed all ideas stated, and calculated the probability that an idea would come from the same category as the idea that was stated just before. A ratio was calculated, namely, the probability of staying in a category over the probability of moving to a new category; interactive groups were much more likely to stay in the same category (ratio = .321 versus .196 for solo individuals).

Fixing Brainstorming

A large body of research has identified the factors that result in productivity loss in interactive brainstorming groups. Further research has shown that these factors can be mitigated by: (1) using a trained facilitator, (2) using electronic brainstorming, and (3) using groups to select ideas.

Trained facilitator

Given the above findings attributing productivity loss to topic fixation, social inhibition, and free riding, a trained facilitator might be able to reduce these factors. Alex Osborn's 1953 book advocated the use of a trained facilitator. At least two studies have found that groups with a trained facilitator are more effective. Offner, Kramer, and Winter (1996) began by training 12 graduate students in effective facilitation techniques, in two sessions of about 2 hours each. They then compared 20 four-person groups with a facilitator, 20 four-person groups with no facilitator, and five nominal groups. They found that the groups with a facilitator generated significantly more ideas than those with no facilitator. Further, they found that groups with a facilitator generated about as many ideas as the nominal groups.

Oxley, Dzindolet, and Paulus (1996) compared the performance of solo individual brainstorming, with groups without a facilitator, and with groups with highly trained (three-hour training), trained (one-hour training), and untrained facilitators (selected at random from the subjects assigned to the group). As with Offner *et al.*, they found that the groups with highly trained facilitators generated as many ideas as nominal group members. They also found that groups with highly trained facilitators outperformed groups with trained and untrained facilitators. In addition, they found one area where the highly trained facilitator outperformed even the nominal group — in the final five minutes of the 20-minute session, the former groups generated almost twice as many ideas as the nominal groups. These findings suggest that if the session were even longer, the groups that had a highly trained facilitator might have significantly out-performed the nominal groups.

Electronic brainstorming

Perhaps the first study of brainstorming where participants interacted via a computer network was in Nunamaker, Applegate, and Konsynski (1987). In the following years, this and other research resulted in a series of software products designed to support group creativity, a software category generally known as *group decision support systems (GDSS)*. A GDSS is generally used with a face-to-face group; each member of the group sits in front of a computer, and all of the computers are networked. Rather than speak ideas out loud, participants type their ideas into their computer; each idea is then immediately displayed on the other participants' screens.

Gallupe, Bastianutti, and Cooper (1991) experimentally tested the system developed by Nunamaker *et al.* (1987), and found that when four-person groups brainstormed using the GDSS, productivity loss did not occur: they generated as many ideas as nominal groups (50 versus 53.20). And electronic brainstorming generated more ideas than face-to-face brainstorming (50 versus 39.80). Gallupe and Cooper (1990) compared the speed of typing an idea to the speed required to say the idea, and found that typing an idea took longer — which should have resulted in reduced productivity for electronic brainstorming, instead of the increased productivity actually observed.

Dennis and Valacich (1993) compared nominal and electronic brainstorming groups of sizes 6 and 12. Consistent with Gallupe *et al.* (1991), they found a non-significant difference in productivity with groups of size 6 (electronic brainstorming 55.42 ideas; nominal 65.81 ideas). However, 12-person electronic brainstorming groups were significantly more productive than 12-person nominal groups, generating 136.44 ideas versus 107.06 ideas. The authors' interpretation, based on observation of these groups in action, was that the electronic brainstorming groups benefited from synergy that resulted from reading each others' ideas. Also, they observed that nominal group members appeared to run out of ideas, generating fewer towards the end of the session, whereas this did not occur in the electronic brainstorming condition.

The increased productivity of electronic brainstorming is consistent with production blocking and with evaluation apprehension (because participants did not know who generated each idea).

Use groups to select ideas

At least one study suggests that groups are better at selecting good ideas than are solitary individuals. After conducting a brainstorming experiment where the task was to "identify uses for a paper clip," Larey (1994) had a different set of subjects evaluate each idea generated and rate their creativity. Judgments were made by interactive groups and by nominal groups. Accuracy of judgments was determined by comparing the creativity ratings of the group or individual with a creativity rating generated by averaging the ratings of ten independent judges. Interactive groups were more accurate than individuals at rating the creativity of the ideas.

Hidden Profiles

One of the hypothesized benefits of groups versus solitary individuals is that groups bring more relevant information to bear on a problem. Each member of the group is likely to have somewhat different information and skills, particularly if the group is composed of members from diverse backgrounds (see section above). So if each member contributes their own unique knowledge to the group discussion, the group collectively would have more information than any one individual, working alone. Wegner's (1986) theory of *transactive memory* suggests that social groups often seek ways to coordinate how they collectively store and use information, and that groups implicitly assign responsibility for sub-domains of information to specific members. The implication of this theory is that many groups succeed by relying on each member having unique information.

However, Stasser and Titus (1985, 2003) found that this hypothesized benefit of groups is rarely realized. They asked four-person teams of college students to evaluate three imaginary candidates for the president of their student body. The candidates were each given attributes and political positions that had previously been identified as desirable, neutral, or undesirable, through an earlier survey of students. Candidate A possessed more desirable traits than the other two (Candidates B and C were identical in their desirability). When a group member received complete profiles of all three candidates, 67% of them chose Candidate A (the remaining third split their votes between B and C). When four students, who all had received the complete profiles, came together in a group and talked about the candidates, 83% of the groups chose Candidate A.

But what happens when no single individual sees the complete profiles? Stasser and Titus (1985) tested two other conditions, where each individual participant had only a subset of the profile information. In a second experiment they called "hidden profile/consensus," each member received a different subset of Candidate A's desirable traits, and a different subset of Candidate B's undesirable traits. As a result, from the perspective of any one member, Candidate B now appeared to have more positive and fewer negative traits than Candidate A — even though collectively, the four team members had the complete information that had enabled them to select Candidate A in the first experiment. A third experiment with a condition Stasser and Titus called "hidden profile/conflict" was similar to "hidden profile/consensus" in how it selectively distributed information to shift support away from Candidate A, except that two of the four team members now received a subset of information that favored Candidate B and the other two received a subset of information that favored Candidate C.

In these hidden profile conditions, pre-discussion votes by each individual member selected Candidate A only 25% of the time. The question is then, when the four team members come together to discuss the candidates, will they exchange their information so that they collectively learn that Candidate A is the best? In fact, just the opposite occurred: in the second experiment (where Candidate B seemed the best initially), after discussion, support for Candidate B *increased* from 61% to 71%. In the third experiment, votes for Candidate A *dropped* after discussion, from 21% to 12%.

The import of these findings is that groups generally fail to share unique information. The practical lesson is that groups should be encouraged to share unique information. However, simply mentioning the unique information is not enough; Stasser, Taylor, and Hanna (1989), and later, Larson *et al.* (1996) found that even if a unique piece of information was shared, it was less likely to be remembered and repeated by other members than was shared information. Stasser and Titus (2003) interpreted these findings as due to the fact that introducing unique information, and repeating unique information, incurs a social cost. In fact, lower status group members were less likely to repeat unique information than high status members (Larson *et al.*, 1996).

Postmes, Spears, and Cihangir (2001) found that priming a group with a "critical thinking norm" rather than a "consensus norm" resulted in a dramatic increase in performance; only 22% of the consensus norm groups selected the best option, but 67% of the critical thinking norm groups did. Galinsky and Kray (2004) found similarly dramatic effects, in a study of groups tasked with solving a mystery, by priming groups with a "counterfactual mindset" that promoted consideration of alternative possibilities; only 23% of the groups without this prime solved the mystery, but 67% of groups with the counterfactual prime solved the mystery. These dramatic effects suggest practical strategies for enhancing group decision making.

3. Norms

Norms are the unwritten rules that govern member behavior within a group (Feldman, 1995). They provide the substance of a group's "climate" or "culture" by suggesting which behaviors are appropriate and encouraged and which behaviors are sanctioned or discouraged (Hackman, 1992). The norms of a group can govern the behavior of individual members within virtually any domain of group functioning. For example, norms may influence how hard, how long, or how carefully members work, the extent to which social relations are encouraged at work, the degree of collaboration and communication between members, etc. In this section, we consider how group norms might affect innovative behavior and outcomes in groups.

Past research has suggested that groups that perform the same work and that operate in the same task or even organizational environment can differ significantly in the extent to which members are engaged in the behaviors and processes associated with innovation (e.g., Argote, Gruenfeld, and Naquin, 2001; Bunderson and Sutcliffe, 2002, 2003;

Edmondson, 1999, 2002; Edmondson, Bohmer, and Pisano, 2001; Gibson and Vermeulen, 2003; Schippers *et al.*, 2003; Van der Vegt and Bunderson, 2005). Bunderson and Sutcliffe (2002, 2003) suggested that these differences are significantly influenced by differences in the learning-related norms that are espoused within a group. In some groups, it is simply expected that members will be actively engaged in experimenting with new ideas, reflecting on past performance, discussing ways of improving team functioning, seeking feedback, etc. Members who engage in these behaviors are celebrated and rewarded (formally or informally) even when, or perhaps especially when, their efforts do not succeed. In contrast, members who adopt passive or reactive approaches to the team's work or who appear content with the status quo are sanctioned (again, formally or informally). Not surprisingly, the evidence suggests that groups that adopt stronger learning norms tend to produce more innovative results (see Drach-Zahavy and Somech, 2001; Ellis *et al.*, 2003).

Given this foundation, a number of researchers have sought to identify factors associated with stronger versus weaker learning norms in teams. In this paper we review three factors that have emerged as robust determinants of learning norms in groups: psychological safety, power asymmetry, and openness to diversity.

Psychological Safety

A number of studies have suggested that in order for learning-related norms and behaviors to emerge in a group, group members need to have a sense of psychological or participative "safety", a confidence that they can engage in risky, learning-related behaviors without punishment or personal disadvantage (Anderson and West, 1998; Baer and Frese, 2003; Bunderson and Boumgarden, 2009; Edmondson, 1999; Nembhard and Edmondson, 2006). In groups with a strong sense of psychological safety, members are more willing to acknowledge mistakes (their own and those of others), point out problems or areas where the team could improve, express opinions, and discuss differences because they are not afraid that those actions will result in negative personal consequences. In contrast, when members are concerned that any of the above actions will negatively impact their relationships with peers or subordinates or their formal or informal standing within the group, they are less likely to speak up. In short, psychological safety is a necessary precondition for the development of strong learning norms within a group.

But how do groups foster psychological safety? Research by Edmondson and colleagues (i.e., Edmondson, 2002; Edmondson, Bohmer, and Pisano, 2001; Nembhard and Edmondson, 2006) suggests that a group leader plays a critical role in fostering psychological safety within a group. Group leaders help to foster psychological safety by, for example, attending to, encouraging, soliciting, and celebrating suggestions and recommendations from all group members and by avoiding any behavior that would signal disapproval of or lack of interest in those contributions. Group leaders can also influence perceptions of psychological safety through the formal incentives established within a group. This finding is consistent with research on organizational culture and climate which suggests that leaders play a critical role in establishing norms and setting the tone for a group or organization (Schein, 1985).

A recent study by Bunderson and Boumgarden (2009) suggests that the formal structure of a group can be another important predictor of both psychological safety and learning norms in groups. In the organizational literature, formal structure is often viewed as an obstacle to innovation. But Bunderson and Boumgarden (2009) found that a clear structure — i.e., clear roles, authority, and rules/procedures — was associated with greater psychological safety, higher supervisor and team member ratings of performance, and a steeper learning curve among production teams in a Fortune 100 high-tech firm. They argue that a clear structure promotes psychological safety by circumventing the suspicions, disagreements, and turf-guarding that arise when member roles and relations are poorly defined.

A study by Bunderson and Sutcliffe (2002) adds an important caveat to the preceding discussion of the important role of psychological safety in promoting learning norms. In a qualitative study of four management teams in a Fortune 100 consumer products company, this study found that an environment of psychological safety was a necessary but not sufficient condition for the emergence of strong learning norms. The more innovative teams in their study not only fostered an environment in which it was safe to take risks, they also fostered an environment in which not taking risks was unacceptable. In other words, while it was perfectly acceptable to try and fail, it was not acceptable not to try, i.e., to be reactive or to be content with the status quo. Bunderson and Sutcliffe conclude that it is this combination of a safe environment that tolerates risks with a normative environment that requires risks that results in the strongest environment for innovation and learning.

Power Asymmetry

Another factor that has been shown to predict learning-related norms in groups is the distribution of intra-group power. Social power in groups is a function of asymmetric control over the resources that group members need in order to do their work (Emerson, 1962), e.g., knowledge, information, access, decision rights, etc. The evidence suggests that the uneven or asymmetric distribution of power within a group can have a stifling effect on group learning norms. So, for example, in a qualitative study of four process improvement teams in a high-tech manufacturing firm, Brooks (1994) found that group reflection and process improvement was virtually absent when even one team member had power over others. A similar study of 12 manufacturing teams by Edmondson (2002) found that in teams where learning and reflection were emphasized, "power differences were either absent or actively minimized" (p. 139). And Eisenhardt and Bourgeois (1988) found that power inequality heightened intra-group politics and undermined team self-improvement in management teams.

Bunderson and Reagans (2009) reviewed the literature on power, status, and learning and articulated three mechanisms by which power asymmetry can stifle learning-related norms and behaviors. First, the evidence suggests that when power differences exist within a team, both high-power and low-power members are less likely to focus on shared group goals and are more likely to engage in defensive and/or politically-motivated behavior. Second, power differences create a more threatening environment for lower-power members (i.e., lower psychological safety) and thereby inhibit risk-taking and experimentation (for the reasons articulated above). And third, power differences impede the open exchange of knowledge and information that is needed for innovation since higher-power people tend to ignore the contributions and knowledge of those lower in the hierarchy. These well-documented tendencies support the conclusion that innovative behavior and power asymmetry may not peacefully coexist in most groups.

A recent study by Van der Vegt *et al.* (2009) notes that this is a problematic conclusion since power differences exist in virtually all teams as a function of member differences in tenure, education, formal authority, etc. If power differences inevitably stifle innovative behavior, it follows that there may be very few truly innovative groups. Van der Vegt *et al.* (2009) question this conclusion, suggesting that perhaps power differences might actually be used to enhance learning if the powerful are motivated to use those power differences for the benefit of the group. They then explore the effect of one specific factor that should influence the group versus individual motivations of the powerful — individual versus group feedback. As hypothesized, they find that power asymmetry actually promoted more innovative, learning-related behaviors in groups where members received feedback as a group, but stifled those behaviors in groups where members received feedback as individuals. This finding suggests that power asymmetries may stifle learning only in cases where the powerful have more individually-oriented motivations.

4. Organizational Context

Teams never operate in a vacuum; each team is part of a broader organizational context. There have been many studies of the features of organizational contexts that result in more innovative teams. As long ago as 1961, Burns and Stalker made the seminal argument that "organic" organizational structures (i.e., decentralized, flexible policies and procedures) are more likely to promote innovation than "mechanistic" organizational structures (i.e., centralized control, formalized procedures). In the classic book *The Social Psychology of Organizing*, management guru Karl Weick similarly argued that smaller, "loosely coupled" organizations are more adaptive than carefully planned organizations. In an influential 1983 book, Henry Mintzberg used the term "adhocracy" to refer to one of five organizational forms, namely, the one with the flattest organizational structures and smaller teams. Management theorists have consistently hypothesized that these looser, more improvisational organizational forms are more innovative (e.g., Quinn, 1985; Mintzberg, 1983; Sawyer, 2007).

Organizational context shapes, directs, and constrains organizational innovation in a variety of ways. But one of the most important means by which organizational context influences innovative activity within an organization is by shaping the way in which organizational members interact, share information, compare knowledge, and combine ideas. In other words, organizational structure and context — the "formal" organization — affects innovation largely by shaping and constraining the "informal" organization, i.e., the network of interactions between and among organization members. For creative problem solving, the informal organization has been shown to matter more than the formal organization (Hargadon and Bechky, 2006). In many highly innovative organizations, innovation emerges from informal teams that emerge outside of the formal organization (Sawyer, 2007). Breakthrough innovations often result when information flows through the informal organization in ways that foster unexpected connections among disparate ideas (Hargadon, 2003).

In recent decades, researchers have made significant strides in assessing and evaluating the informal organization through the use of *social network analysis* (SNA). A social network consists of a set of nodes, each representing an individual, and links between nodes, representing a relationship. These relationships have been conceived in different ways. First, a network link or "tie" could be defined in terms of its strength (Granovetter, 1973). Stronger ties are characterized by more emotional closeness, more frequent and longer interactions, and mutual and reciprocated judgments of the importance of the relationship (Hansen, 1999; Wegener, 1991). (Some researchers have suggested that these may be distinct dimensions of tie strength, and may have different outcomes: Marsden and Campbell, 1984; Perry-Smith, 2006.) Second, a network tie could be defined in terms of the content of communication. Are people exchanging advice? Political support? Information needed to complete a task?

One of the most solid findings of SNA is that strong friendships are not good for creativity. This may seem counter-intuitive; but it is because: (1) we tend to have close relationships to people who are like us, and (2) our good friends typically know each other. As a result, social networks strong in friendship tend to be groups where everyone knows each other, and where individual knowledge and attitudes tend to converge over time (Burt, 1992). Thus, it is less likely that one will encounter a surprising new viewpoint from a close friend — and hearing the same views and the same information that one already holds does not contribute to creativity (Perry-Smith, 2006; see above section on turnover in teams).

In contrast, so-called *weak ties* — where two people are linked, but not very strongly — are more strongly associated with creativity (Perry-Smith and Shalley, 2003). In contrast to strong ties, weak ties are where people interact only infrequently, and for shorter durations each time. A person is more likely to acquire new information from a weak tie than from a strong tie, because strongly connected nodes tend to have the same sources and share the same information. Furthermore, a weak tie does not require a strong emotional bond, and as a result, individuals may be more tolerant of differences (Coser, 1975; Granovetter, 1982). Strong ties are more typical between similar people (Ibarra, 1992; Lincoln and Miller, 1979; McPherson, Smith-Lovin, and Cook, 2001). In a study of an applied research institute, Perry-Smith (2006) found that individuals with more ties with other researchers were more creative.

Thus, weak ties facilitate creativity by: (1) providing a greater amount and diversity of new information that is related to an ongoing problem; (2) providing exposure to cognitive diversity — different approaches and perspectives. Several studies support these claims:

• In a study of 772 artists, Simonton (1984) found that more distant relationships were associated with greater artistic eminence. The most creative artists were those with connections to highly distinguished artists, which Simonton called *paragons*. And in general, artists were more creative if they lived during a period with more living paragons — suggesting that simple exposure to exceptional creators enhances creativity. There is some evidence that this finding extends to organizational contexts. Zhou (2003) found that individuals were more creative when they had more creative coworkers. This relationship was stronger for individuals who started out being less creative. The causal mechanism seems to be modeling: individuals learn creative behaviors and ways of thinking by observing others who are effectively creative (Shalley and Perry-Smith, 2001).

- Perry-Smith (2006), in a study of an applied research institute, found that individuals with many acquaintances, rather than a few close colleagues, were more creative.

- In a study of a Scandinavian telecommunications company, Rodan and Galunic (2004) found that managers who were connected to other managers with different knowledge bases were more innovative.

Burt (1992) introduced the seminal concept of the *structural hole* in order to capture the benefits that individuals derive from these weak ties. Imagine an organization with two distinct work groups. If there is no contact between the two groups, this creates a *structural hole*: an opportunity for an individual to connect to both groups, and thus act as an *information broker* between the two groups. Burt (1992) argued that individuals who occupy these structural holes gain power and hold unique information. They are promoted faster, and they receive larger bonuses. Moreover, ideas from individuals who occupy structural holes are judged to be more innovative (Burt, 2004). And, when structural holes are filled, an organization is more able to accept new ideas (Burt, 2004).

The opposite of a loosely connected organizational network would be a network where all ties are strong ties, and where the same people are all connected to each other. This sort of network is referred to as *densely connected*. Managers with dense networks have been found to be less adaptable, and less likely to modify their networks when the task environment changes (Gargiulo and Benassi, 2000).

Uzzi and Spiro (2005) analyzed a network of 2,092 people who worked on 474 musicals between 1945 and 1989. They analyzed the creative success of each musical using measures like critics' reviews and financial success. For each musical, a unique team of six freelance individuals is brought together: a composer, a lyricist, a libbretist (who writes the plot and dialogue), a choreographer, a director, and a producer. The strength of a tie between two of these professionals was measured by how many musicals overall they had worked on together. Uzzi and Spiro found an inverse U relationship between connectedness of a team and musical success; up to a point, increased connectedness resulted in increased success, and beyond that point, an increase in connectedness negatively impacted creative success.

In sum, social network analyses have converged on the finding that both too-dense and too-unconnected networks are bad for creativity; the ideal network is one that has both dense connections and loose connections, and is often referred to as a *small world network*. (Note the connections with the above section on turnover in teams.)

Teams and Creativity

The above findings seem to be in tension with findings in team research that highly cohesive teams are more effective — because a highly cohesive team is, by definition, densely connected. Highly cohesive teams have more satisfied group members and greater consensus (Beal *et al.*, 2003; Sethi, Smith, and Park, 2001). A meta-analysis by Balkundi and Harrison (2006) found that teams with dense interpersonal networks were better at attaining their goals, and that when team leaders were more central in the group's network, the team performed better.

Given the above research, however, we might expect that more cohesive teams are less creative. There is one study that suggests this is the case (Perry-Smith and Shalley, 2003) — that instead, groups with weak ties with one another are more creative. And a host of studies have found that teams with high degrees of consensus are more prone to make bad decisions, because of the risk of *group think* (Janis, 1972). A second tradition of research has found that there is no relationship between a group's member satisfaction and its effectiveness; for example, even though brainstorming groups generate fewer ideas than comparison nominal groups, the brainstorming group's members are much more satisfied, and even believe that they are more creative, a phenomenon known as *the illusion of group effectiveness* (Paulus, Larey, and Ortega, 1995).

When team members have weak external ties, the team is more likely to be creative. Ancona and Caldwell (1992) found that socially isolated teams were not very innovative, compared to teams with informal relationships outside the team. Weak external ties can help a team gain political support and acquire resources, but they can also work as conduits for the flow of diverse information (Ancona and Bresman, 2007; Cummings, 2004; Hansen, 1999; Tushman, 1977). These weak ties increase the likelihood that a team can think in more flexible ways and come up with a broader range of unique solutions to problems. Individuals with outside connections are more likely to receive new information and new perspectives (Fleming and Marx, 2006). Sutton and Hargadon (1996) argued that certain types of firms, such as design consultancies, prosper by acting as *knowledge brokers* — their entire business model is premised on many weak ties to a wide range of organizations.

Centrality

In addition to an individual's pattern of network links, there is a large body of research that an individual's location within the overall organizational network is important to promotion, advancement, and power (Blau and Alba, 1982; Brass, 1984, 1992; Cross and Cummings, 2004; Sparrowe *et al.*, 2001). Imagine a large social network, with several hundred nodes, and all of the links between the nodes mapped out. Although two different individuals may both have the same number of links, one individual's links may be more strategically placed — they may be more *central*. "Centrality" refers to the degree to which a person is in the middle of the network, loosely speaking. There are at least three ways to define the centrality of a node: (1) the number of contacts; (2) betweenness, or the extent to which a node falls between pairs of other points on the shortest path between them; and (3) *closeness centrality*, a measure of the average of the shortest distances to all other nodes in the network, so that the person who can reach the largest number of others with the fewest links is more central. This third measure of closeness is the one most frequently used; a more closeness central node can reach other nodes through a minimum number of intermediary nodes and is therefore dependent on fewer intermediary positions, and thus it measures the degree of independent access to others. Brass (1984) found that higher centrality individuals, measured using closeness, were more likely to be promoted and were rated as more influential.

Research is inconclusive on the link between centrality and creativity. On the one hand, it might seem that centrality would lead to less creativity; after all, research suggests that more densely connected individuals are less creative and less adaptive, and being more central seems related to dense links. On the other hand, greater centrality might result in a broader range of perspectives, and access to a wider variety of organizational subcultures, which would enhance creativity. Some research suggests that centrality is related to the ability to successfully "sell" a novel idea (Fleming and Marx, 2006; Mehra, Kilduff, and Brass, 2001; Obstfeld, 2005). As long ago as Rogers (1962), network centrality has been associated with the successful diffusion of a new idea. Although Burt (2004), in widely cited research, found that structural holes lead to good ideas, there was no evidence that these good ideas were actually implemented in successful products or processes. The problem is that by definition, individuals who occupy structural holes, after they have a good idea by combining distinct bodies of knowledge, have the difficult task of bringing together very different groups of individuals to turn that idea into a reality. Obstfeld (2005), in a study of an engineering division of a car company, found that engineers who worked to bring together disconnected people were more likely to be involved with successful innovation.

5. Putting the Framework into Practice

Social ties can help people be more creative, can help teams be more creative, and can help organizations be more innovative. The research reviewed above identifies several characteristics of social networks that are associated with enhanced creativity.

At the individual level, it is best to be connected but not too connected. It is best to have some number of weak ties, in addition to the strong ties that characterize most work teams and organizational units. Individuals should also seek to develop ties outside of their local, dense network.

At the team level, although team cohesion is associated with greater work satisfaction and efficiency, it runs the risk of reducing team creativity. Team members should make sure to remain connected outside of their team. (See team diversity section of this review.) Team leaders should:

- provide incentives to members who bring information from external ties;
- give time in the schedule for these ties to be pursued;
- watch out for too much cohesiveness.

At the organization level, a small world structure is more innovative than either a network with all dense ties, or a network with exclusively weak ties. Organization leaders can increase the likelihood of a small world structure by:

- frequent reassignment of staff (see the above review of turnover and innovation);
- innovation labs;
- shadowing staff in another unit;
- incentive systems that reward cross-unit contacts and exchange of information;
- office space architecture that increases the likelihood of encounters with different others that might lead to a weak tie being formed.

6. Conclusion

Organizational behavior scholars have contributed greatly to our understanding of creativity and innovation in organizations. Most of these contributions have focused on teams and organizations, rather than on individual creativity; individual creativity has been studied within the discipline of psychology rather than organizational behavior. Our review has focused on teams and innovation, reflecting a focus in the field on this level of analysis. We also reviewed recent studies using the new methodology of social network analysis, because these have strong implications for our understanding of innovation in teams and in organizations.

Future studies are necessary to connect our current knowledge across the three levels of analysis of individuals, teams, and organizations. What are the mechanisms whereby certain team designs enhance or detract from an individual member's creativity? How can a particular organizational culture affect team formation and effectiveness? The field also needs research on how broader contextual factors influence team and individual creativity — factors in the national innovation system, such as tax policy, the educational system, and the intellectual property regime. Such studies are likely to require interdisciplinary teams combining expertise in psychology, group dynamics, organizations, and national policy.

References

Aldag, R. J. and Fuller, S. R. (1993). Beyond fiasco: A Reappraisal of the Group Think Phenomenon and a New Model of Group Decision Processes. *Psychological Bulletin*, 113: 533–552.

Ancona, D. and Bresman, H. (2007). *X-teams: How to Build Teams that Lead, Innovate, and Succeed.* Boston, MA: Harvard Business School Press.

Ancona, D. G. and Caldwell, D. F. (1992). Demography and Design: Predictors of New Product Team Performance. *Organization Science*, 3: 321–341.

Anderson, N. R. and West, M. A. (1998). Measuring Climate for Work Group Innovation: Development and Validation of the Team Climate Inventory. *J. of Organ. Behavior*, 19: 235–258.

Argote, L., Insko, C. A., Yovetich, N. and Romero, A. A. (1995). Group learning curves: The effects of turnover and task complexity on group performance. *Journal of Applied Social Psychology*, 25: 512–529.

Argote, L., Gruenfeld, D. and Naquin, C. (2001). Group Learning in Organizations. In M. E. Turner (Ed.), *Groups at Work: Theory and Research* (pp. 369–411). Mahwah, NJ: Lawrence Erlbaum.

Arrow, H. and McGrath, J. E. (1993). How Member Change and Continuity Affects Small Group Structure, Process, and Performance. *Small Group Research*, 24: 334–361.

Arrow, H. and McGrath, J. E. (1995). Membership Dynamics in Groups at Work: A Theoretical Framework. *Research in Organizational Behavior*, 17: 373–411.

Baer, M. and Frese, M. (2003). Innovation is not Enough: Climates for Initiative and Psychological Safety, Process Innovations, and Firm Performance. *J. of Organ. Behavior*, 24: 45–68.

Balkundi, P. and Harrison, D. A. (2006). Ties, Leaders, and Time in Teams: Strong Inference About Network Structure's Effects on Team Viability and Performance. *Academy of Management Journal*, 49: 49–68.

Bantel, K. A. and Jackson, S. E. (1989). Top Management and Innovations in Banking: Does the Demography of the Top Team Make a Difference? *Strategic Management Journal*, 10: 107–124.

Beal, D. J., Cohen, R. R., Burke, M. J. and McLendon, C. L. (2003). Cohesion and Performance in Groups: A Meta-Analytic Clarification of Construct Relations. *Journal of Applied Psychology*, 88: 989–1004.

Blau, J. R. and Alba, R. D. (1982). Empowering Nets of Participation. *Administrative Science Quarterly*, 27: 363–379.

Bouchard, T. J. (1972). A Comparison of Two Group Brainstorming Procedures. *Journal of Applied Psychology*, 56: 418–421.

Bouchard, T. J. and Hare, M. (1970). Size, Performance, and Potential in Brainstorming Groups. *Journal of Applied Psychology*, 54(1): 51–55.

Brass, D. J. (1984). Being in the Right Place: A Structural Analysis of Individual Influence in an Organization. *Administrative Science Quarterly*, 29: 518–539.

Brass, D. J. (1992). Power in Organizations: A Social Network Perspective. In G. Moore and J. A. Whitt (Eds.), *Research in Politics and Society* (pp. 295–323). Greenwich, CT: JAI Press.

Brooks, A. (1994). Power and the Production of Knowledge: Collective Team Learning in Work Organizations. *Human Resource Development Quarterly*, 5: 213–235.

Bunderson, J. S. and Boumgarden, P. (2009). Structure and Learning in Self-Managed Teams: Why 'Bureaucratic' Teams can be Better Learners. In Press at *Organization Science*.

Bunderson, J. S. and Reagans, R. E. (2009). Power, Status, and Learning in Organizations. Forthcoming in *Organization Science*.

Bunderson, J. S. and Sutcliffe, K. M. (2002). Why Some Teams Emphasize Learning More Than Others: Evidence From Business Unit Management Teams. H. Sondak, vol. ed., E. A. Mannix, M. A. Neale, series eds., *Research on Managing Groups and Teams: Vol. 4. Toward phenomenology of groups and group membership* (pp. 49–84). Oxford, England: Elsevier Science.

Bunderson, J. S. and Sutcliffe, K. M. (2003). Management Team Learning Orientation and Business Unit Performance. *J. of Applied Psych.*, 88: 552–560.

Burns, T. and Stalker, G. M. (1961). *The Management of Innovation.* London: Tavistock.

Burt, R. S. (1982). *Toward a Structural Theory of Action: Network Models of Social Structure, Perception, and Action.* New York: Academic Press.

Burt, R. S. (1992). *Structural Holes.* Cambridge, MA: Harvard University Press.

Burt, R. S. (2004). Structural Holes and Good Ideas. *American Journal of Sociology*, 110: 349–399.

Choi, H. S. and Levine, J. M. (2004). Minority Influence in Work Teams: The Impact of Newcomers. *Journal of Experimental Social Psychology*, 40(2): 273–280.

Collaros, P. A. and Anderson, L. R. (1969). Effect of Perceived Expertness Upon Creativity of Members of Brainstorming Groups. *Journal of Applied Psychology*, 53: 159–163.

Coser, R. (1975). The Complexity of Roles as a Seedbed of Individual Autonomy. In L. A. Coser (Ed.), *The Idea of Social Structure: Papers in Honor of Robert K. Merton* (pp. 237–263). New York: Harcourt Brace.

Cross, R. and Cummings, J. N. (2004). Tie and Network Correlates of Individual Performance in Knowledge-Intensive Work. *Academy of Management Journal*, 47(6): 928–937.

Cummings, J. (2004). Work Groups, Structural Diversity, and Knowledge Sharing in a Global Organization. *Management Science*, 50: 352–364.

Dalton, D. R. (1997). Employee Transfer and Employee Turnover: A Theoretical and Practical Disconnect? *Journal of Organizational Behavior*, 18: 411–413.

Dennis, A. R. and Valacich, J. S. (1993). Computer Brainstorms: More Heads are Better Than One. *Journal of Applied Psychology*, 78(4): 531–537.

Diehl, M. and Stroebe, W. (1987). Productivity Loss in Brainstorming Groups: Toward the Solution of a Riddle. *Journal of Personality and Social Psychology*, 53(3): 497–509.

Diehl, M. and Stroebe, W. (1991). Productivity Loss in Idea-Generating Groups: Tracking Down the Blocking Effect. *Journal of Personality and Social Psychology*, 61: 392–403.

Drach-Zahavy, A. and Somech, A. (2001). Understanding Team Innovation: The Role of Team Processes and Structures. *Group Dynamics: Theory, Research, and Practice*, 5: 111–123.

Edmondson, A. C. (1999). Psychological Safety and Learning Behavior in Work Teams. *Admin. Sci. Quart.*, 44: 350–383.

Edmondson, A. C. (2002). The Local and Variegated Nature of Learning in Organizations: A Group-Level Perspective. *Organ. Sci.*, 13: 128–146.

Edmondson, A. C., Bohmer, R. M. and Pisano, G. P. (2001). Disrupted Routines: Team Learning and New Technology Implementation in Hospitals. *Admin. Sci. Quart.*, 46: 685–716.

Eisenhardt, K. M. and Bourgeois, L. J. (1988). Politics of Strategic Decision-Making in High-Velocity Environments: Toward a Midrange Theory. *Academy of Management Journal*, 31: 737–770.

Ellis, A. P. J., Hollenbeck, J. R., Ilgen, D. R., Porter, C. O. L. H., West, B. J. and Moon, H. (2003). Team Learning: Collectively Connecting the Dots. *J. of Applied Psych.*, 88: 821–835.

Emerson, R. M. (1962). Power-Dependence Relations. *American Sociological Review*, 27: 31–41.

Feldman, D. C. (1995). Group norms. In N. Nicholson, R. Schuler, and A. H. Van de Ven (Eds.), *Blackwell Encyclopedic Dictionary of Organizational Behavior* (pp. 204–205). Cambridge, MA: Blackwell Business.

Fleming, L. and Marx, M. (2006). Managing Creativity in Small Worlds. *California Management Review*, 48(4): 6–26.

Galinsky, A. and Kray, L. J. (2004). From Thinking About What Might have been to Sharing What We Know: The Role of Counterfactual Mind-Sets on Information Sharing in Groups. *Journal of Experimental Social Psychology*, 40: 606–618.

Gallupe, R. B., Bastianutti, L. M. and Cooper, W. H. (1991). Unblocking Brainstorms. *Journal of Applied Psychology*, 76: 137–142.

Gallupe, R. B. and Cooper, W. H. (1990). Average Time to Speak vs. Keyboard Ideas [Unpublished Raw Data]. Queen's University School of Business, Kingston, Ontario, Canada.

Gargiulo, M. and Benassi, M. (2000). Trapped in Your Own Net? Network Cohesion, Structural Holes, and the Adaptation of Social Capital. *Organization Science*, 11: 183–196.

George, J. M. (2007). Creativity in Organizations. *The Academy of Management Annals*, 1(1): 439–477.

Gibson, C. and Vermeulen, F. (2003). A Healthy Divide: Subgroups as a Stimulus for Team Learning Behavior. *Admin. Sci. Quart.*, 48: 202–239.

Granovetter, M. (1973). The Strength of Weak Ties. *American Journal of Sociology*, 6: 1360–1380.

Granovetter, M. (1982). The Strength of Weak Ties: A Network Theory Revisited. In P. V. Marsden and N. Lin (Eds.), *Social Structure and Network Analysis* (pp. 105–130). Beverly Hills, CA: Sage.

Gruenfeld, D. H., Martorana, P. V. and Fan, E. T. (2000). What Do Groups Learn from their Worldliest Members? Direct and Indirect Influence in Dynamic Teams. *Organizational Behavior and Human Decision Processes*, 82(1): 45–59.

Hackman, J. R. (1992). Group Influences on Individuals in Organizations. In M. D. Dunnette and L. M. Hough (Eds.), *Handbook of Industrial and Organizational Psychology*, Vol. 3, 2nd ed. (pp. 199–267). Palo Alto, CA, US: Consulting Psychologists Press.

Hambrick, D. C., Cho, T. and Chen, M. (1996). The Influence of Top Management Team Heterogeneity on Firms' Competitive Moves. *Administrative Science Quarterly*, 41: 659–684.

Hansen, M. T. (1999). The search-transfer problem: The Role of Weak Ties in Sharing Knowledge Across Organizational Sub-Units. *Administrative Science Quarterly*, 37: 422–447.

Hargadon, A. B. (2003). *How Breakthroughs Happen: The Surprising Truth About How Companies Innovate*. Boston, MA: Harvard Business School Press.

Hargadon, A. B. and Bechky, B. A. (2006). When Collections of Creatives Become Creative Collections: A Field Study of Problem Solving at Work. *Organization Science*, 17: 484–500.

Hyams, N. B. and Graham, W. K. (1984). Effects of Goal Setting and Initiative on Individual Brainstorming. *Journal of Social Psychology*, 123: 283–284.

Ibarra, H. (1992). Homophily and Differential Returns: Sex Differences in Network Structure and Access in an Advertising Firm. *Administrative Science Quarterly*, 37: 277–303.

Janis, I. L. (1972). *Victims of Groupthink: A Psychological Study of Foreign-Policy Decisions and Fiascos*. Boston: Houghton Mifflin Company.

Jehn, K. A., Northcraft, G. B. and Neale, M. A. (1999). Why Differences Make a Difference: A Field Study of Diversity, Conflict, and Performance in Work Groups. *Administrative Science Quarterly*, 44: 741–763.

Kane, A. A., Argote, L. and Levine, J. M. (2005). Knowledge Transfer Between Groups via Personnel Rotation: Effects of Social Identity and Knowledge Quality. *Organizational Behavior and Human Decision Processes*, 96: 56–71.

Kanter, R. M. (1988). When a Thousand Flowers Bloom: Structural, Collective, and Social Conditions for Innovation in Organizations. In B. M. Staw and L. L. Cummings (Eds.), *Research in Organization Behavior*, Vol. 10 (pp. 169–211). Greenwich, CT: JAI Press.

Katz, R. (1982). The Effects of Group Longevity on Project Communication and Performance. *Admin. Sci. Quart.*, 27: 81–104.

Keck, S. L. (1997). Top Management Team Structure: Differential Effects By Environmental Context. *Organization Science*, 8(2): 143–156.

Kelley, T. (2001). *The Art of Innovation: Lessons in Creativity from IDEO, America's Leading Design Firm*. New York: Doubleday.

Kerr, H. L. and Bruun, S. E. (1983). The Dispensability of Member Effort and Group Motivation Losses: Free Rider Effects. *Journal of Personality and Social Psychology*, 44: 78–94.

Knight, D., Pearce, C. L., Smith, K. G., Olian, J. D., Sims, H. P., Smith, K. A. and Flood, P. (1999). Top Management Team Diversity, Group Process, and Strategic Consensus. *Strategic Management Journal*, 20: 445–465.

Kozlowski, S. W. J. and Bell, B. S. (2003). Work Groups and Teams in Organizations. In W. C. Borman, D. R. Ilgen and R. J. Klimoski (Eds.), *Handbook of Psychology, Volume 12: Industrial and organizational psychology* (pp. 333–375). New York: Wiley.

Kozlowski, S. W. J. and Ilgen, D. R. (2006). Enhancing the Effectiveness of Work Groups and Teams. *Psychological Science in the Public Interest*, 7(3): 77–124.

Lant, T. K., Milliken, F. J. and Batra, B. (1992). The Role of Managerial Learning and Interpretation in Strategic Persistence and Reorientation: An Empirical Exploration. *Strategic Management Journal*, 13: 585–608.

Larey, T. S. (1994). *Convergent and divergent thinking, group composition, and creativity in brainstorming groups*. Unpublished Doctoral Dissertation, University of Texas, Arlington.

Larey, T. S. and Paulus, P. B. (1999). Group Preference and Convergent Tendencies in Small Groups: A Content Analysis of Group Brainstorming Performance. *Creativity Research Journal*, 12(3): 175–184.

Larson, J. R., Christiansen, C., Abbott, A. S. and Franz, T. M. (1996). Diagnosing Groups: Charting the Flow of Information in Medical Decision Making Teams. *Journal of Personality and Social Psychology*, 71: 315–330.

Levine, J. M., Choi, H. S. and Moreland, R. L. (2003). Newcomer Innovation in Work Teams. In P. B. Paulus and B. A. Nijstad (Eds.), *Group Creativity: Innovation Through Collaboration* (pp. 202–224). New York: Oxford University Press.

Lincoln, J. R. and Miller, J. (1979). Work and Friendship Ties in Organizations: A Comparative Analysis of Relational Networks. *Administrative Science Quarterly*, 24: 181–199.

Maginn, B. K. and Harris, R. J. (1980). Effects of Anticipated Evaluation on Individual Brainstorming Performance. *Journal of Applied Psychology*, 65: 219–225.

Mannix, E. and Neale, M. A. (2005). What Difference Makes a Difference? The Promise and Reality of Diverse Teams in Organizations. *Psychological Science*, 6(2): 31–55.

Marsden, P. V. and Campbell, K. E. (1984). Measuring Tie Strength. *Social Forces*, 63: 482–501.

McPherson, M., Smith-Lovin, L. and Cook, J. M. (2001). Birds of a Feather: Homophily in Social Networks. *Annual Review of Sociology*, 27: 415–444.

Mehra, A., Kilduff, M. and Brass, D. J. (2001). The Social Networks of High and Low Self-Monitors: Implications for Workplace Performance. *Administrative Science Quarterly*, 46: 121–146.

Milliken, F. and Martins, L. (1996). Searching for Common Threads: Understanding the Multiple Effects of Diversity in Organizational Groups. *Academy of Management Review*, 21(2): 402–433.

Mintzberg, H. (1983). *Structure in Fives: Designing Effective Organizations.* Englewood Cliffs, NJ: Prentice-Hall.

Moreland, R. L. and Levine, J. M. (2002). Socialization and Trust in Work Groups. *Group Processes and Intergroup Relations*, 5: 185–201.

Mullen, B., Johnson, C. and Salas, E. (1991). Productivity Loss in Brainstorming Groups: A Meta-Analytic Integration. *Basic and Applied Social Psychology*, 12(1): 3–23.

Nembhard, I. M. and Edmondson, A. C. (2006). Making it Safe: The Effects of Leader Inclusiveness and Professional Status on Psychological Safety and Improvement Efforts in Health Care Teams. *J. of Organ. Behavior*, 27: 941–966.

Nemeth, C. (1986). Differential Contributions of Majority and Minority Influence. *Psychological Review*, 93(1): 23–32.

Nunamaker, J. F., Applegate, L. M. and Konsynski, B. R. (1987). Facilitating Group Creativity: Experience with a Group Decision Support System. *Journal of Management Information Systems*, 3: 5–19.

O'Connor, K. M., Gruenfeld, D. H. and McGrath, J. E. (1993). The Experience and Effects of Conflict in Continuing Work Groups. *Small Group Research*, 24: 362–382.

Obstfeld, D. (2005). Social Networks, the *Tertius Iungens* Orientation, and Involvement in Innovation. *Administrative Science Quarterly*, 50: 100–130.

Offner, A. K., Kramer, T. J. and Winter, J. P. (1996). The Effects of Facilitation, Recording, and Pauses on Group Brainstorming. *Small Group Research*, 27(2): 283–298.

Osborn, A. F. (1953). *Applied Imagination*. Buffalo, NY: Creative Education Foundation Press.

Oxley, N. L., Dzindolet, M. T. and Paulus, P. B. (1996). The Effects of Facilitators on the Performance of Brainstorming Groups. *Journal of Social Behavior and Personality*, 11(4): 633–646.

Paulus, P. B. and Dzindolet, M. T. (1993). Social Influence Processes in Group Brainstorming. *Journal of Personality and Social Psychology*, 64: 575–586.

Paulus, P. B., Larey, T. S. and Ortega, A. H. (1995). Performance and Perceptions of Brainstormers in an Organizational Setting. *Basic and Applied Social Psychology*, 17: 249–265.

Pelled, L. H., Eisenhardt, K. M. and Xin, K. R. (1999). Exploring the Black Box: An Analysis of Work Group Diversity, Conflict, and Performance. *Administrative Science Quarterly*, 44: 1–28.

Perry-Smith, J. E. (2006). Social yet creative: The Role of Social Relationships in Facilitating Individual Creativity. *Academy of Management Journal*, 49: 85–101.

Perry-Smith, J. E. and Shalley, C. E. (2003). The Social Side of Creativity: A Static and Dynamic Social Network Perspective. *Academy of Management Review*, 28: 89–106.

Postmes, T., Spears, R. and Cihangir, S. (2001). Quality of Decision Making and Group Norms. *Journal of Personality and Social Psychology*, 80: 918–930.

Quinn, J. B. (1985). Managing Innovation: Controlled Chaos. *Harvard Business Review*, 63: 73–80.

Rodan, S. and Galunic, D. C. (2004). More Than Network Structure: How Knowledge Heterogeneity Influences Managerial Performance and Innovativeness. *Strategic Management Journal*, 25: 541–562.

Rogers, E. M. (1962). *Diffusion of Innovations*. New York: Free Press of Glencoe.

Runco, M. A. (2004). Creativity. *Annual Review of Psychology*, 55: 657–687.

Sawyer, R. K. (2007). *Group Genius: The Creative Power of Collaboration*. New York: BasicBooks.

Schein, E. (1985). *Organizational Culture and Leadership*. San Francisco: Jossey-Bass.

Schippers, M. C., Den Hartog, D. N., Koopman, P. L. and Wienk, J. A. (2003). Diversity and Team Outcomes: The Moderating Effects of Outcome Interdependence and Group Longevity and the Mediating Effect of Reflexivity. *J. of Organ. Behavior*, 24: 779–802.

Sethi, R., Smith, D. C. and Park, C. W. (2001). Cross-Functional Product Development Teams, Creativity, and the Innovativeness of Consumer Products. *Journal of Marketing Research*, 38: 73–85.

Shalley, C. E. and Perry-Smith, J. E. (2001). Effects of Social-Psychological Factors on Creative Performance: The Role of Informational and Controlling Expected Evaluation and Modeling Experience. *Organizational Behavior and Human Decision Processes*, 84: 1–22.

Shalley, C. E., Zhou, J. and Oldham, G. R. (2004). Effects of Personal and Contextual Characteristics on Creativity: Where Should We Go From Here? *Journal of Management*, 30: 933–958.

Shaw, J. D., Duffy, M. K., Johnson, J. L. and Lockhart, D. E. (2005). Turnover, Social Capital Losses, and Performance. *Academy of Management Journal*, 48: 594–606.

Simonton, D. K. (1984). Artistic Creativity and Interpersonal Relationships Across and Within Generations. *Journal of Personality and Social Psychology*, 46: 1273–1286.

Sparrowe, R. T., Liden, R. C., Wayne, S. J. and Kraimer, M. L. (2001). Social Networks and the Performance of Individuals and Groups. *Academy of Management Journal*, 44(2): 316–325.

Stasser, G., Taylor, L. A. and Hanna, C. (1989). Information Sampling in Structured and Unstructured Discussions of Three- and Six-Person Groups. *Journal of Personality and Social Psychology*, 57: 67–78.

Stasser, G. and Titus, W. (1985). Pooling of Unshared Information in Group Decision Making: Biased Information Sampling During Discussion. *Journal of Personality and Social Psychology*, 48: 1467–1478.

Stasser, G. and Titus, W. (2003). Hidden Profiles: A Brief History. *Psychological Inquiry*, 14(3&4): 304–313.

Steiner, I. D. (1972). *Group Processes and Productivity*. New York: Academic Press.

Stroebe, W. and Diehl, M. (1994). Why Groups are Less Effective Than Their Members: On Productivity Losses in Idea-Generating Groups. *European Review of Social Psychology*, 5: 271–303.

Stroebe, W. and Frey, B. S. (1982). Self-Interest and Collective Action: The Economics and Psychology of Public Goods. *British Journal of Social Psychology*, 21: 121–137.

Sutton, R. I. and Hargadon, A. B. (1996). Brainstorming Groups in Context: Effectiveness in a Product Design Firm. *Administrative Science Quarterly*, 41: 685–718.

Taylor, D. W., Berry, P. C. and Block, C. H. (1958). Does Group Participation When Using Brainstorming Facilitate or Inhibit Creative Thinking? *Administrative Science Quarterly*, 3(1): 23–47.

Tsui, A. S., Egan, T. D. and Xin, K. R. (1995). Diversity in Organizations: Lessons from Demography Research. In M. M. Chemers, S. Oskamp, and M. A. Costanzo (Eds.), *Diversity in Organizations: New Perspectives for a Changing Workplace* (pp. 191–219). Thousand Oaks, CA: Sage.

Tushman, M. L. (1977). Special Boundary Roles in the Innovation Process. *Administrative Science Quarterly*, 22: 587–605.

Uzzi, B. and Spiro, J. (2005). Collaboration and Creativity: The Small World Problem. *American Journal of Sociology*, 111(2): 447–504.

Van der Vegt, G. S. and Bunderson, J. S. (2005). Learning and Performance in Multidisciplinary Teams: The Importance of Collective Team Identification. *Acad. of Management J.*, 48: 532–547.

Van der Vegt, G. S., Bunderson, J. S. and Kuipers, B. (2009). Why Turnover Matters in Self-Managing Work Teams: Learning, Social Integration, and Task Flexibility. In Press at *Journal of Management*.

Van der Vegt, G. S., de Jong, S. B., Bunderson, J. S. and Molleman, E. (2009). Power Asymmetry and Learning in Teams: The Moderating Role of Performance Feedback. In Press at *Organization Science*.

Virany, B., Tushman, M. L. and Romanelli, E. (1992). Executive Succession and Organization Outcomes in Turbulent Environments: An Organizational Learning Approach. *Organization Science*, 3: 72–91.

Wegener, B. (1991). Job Mobility and Social Ties: Social Resources, Prior Job, and Status Attainment. *American Sociological Review*, 56: 60–71.

Wegner, D. M. (1986). Transactive memory: A Contemporary Analysis of the Group Mind. In B. Mullen and G. Goethals (Eds.), *Theories of Group Behavior* (pp. 185–208). New York: Springer-Verlag.

Weick, K. E. (1969). *The Social Psychology of Organizing*. Reading, MA: Addison-Wesley.

Wiersema, M. F. and Bantel, K. A. (1992). Top Management Team Demography and Corporate Strategic Change. *Academy of Management Journal*, 35: 91–121.

Zhou, J. (2003). When the Presence of Creative Coworkers is Related to Creativity: Role of Supervisor Close Monitoring, Developmental Feedback, and Creative Personality. *Journal of Applied Psychology*, 88: 413–422.

Zhou, J. and Shalley, C. E. (2003). Research on Employee Creativity: A Critical Review and Directions for Future Research. *Research in Personnel and Human Resource Management*, 22: 165–217.

Ziller, R. C., Behringer, R. D. and Goodchilds, J. (1962). Group Creativity Under Conditions of Success or Failure and Variations in Group Stability. *Journal of Applied Psychology*, 46: 43–49.

Chapter 3

Managing Innovation Processes and New Product Development Projects: Operations and Marketing Research Perspectives

Panos Kouvelis

Emerson Distinguished Professor of Operations and Manufacturing Management, Olin Business School, Washington University in St. Louis; Director, Boeing Center for Technology, Information and Manufacturing

Betul Lus

Assistant Professor of Decision Sciences, School for Graduate Studies, SUNY Empire State College

Most businesses today are under the intense pressure of highly competitive markets combined with shortened product lifecycles. The future growth and survival of these businesses heavily relies on their ability to quickly develop and bring new products to the market or to redesign their existing product lines to meet new market requirements. However, successful and effective introduction of new products is becoming more challenging than ever in recent years due to increased fierce competition and rapid market changes. In this chapter, we discuss the emerging opportunities and challenges that companies face in new product development focusing on the selected topics of platform-based product development, disruptive innovation, portfolio management and resource allocation, and incentives. We provide a review of literature on innovation and new product development in the fields of marketing and operations management and present the most impactful research results and findings on the theory and practice of effective innovation and product development. We also point out knowledge gaps that new research needs to fill.

1. Introduction

In today's highly competitive and rapidly changing market, successful new product development (NPD) is crucial for the survival and growth of companies. Based on the fact that almost 30% of companies' sales are from new products, the development of new products becomes essential to the success of businesses. New product development is an increasingly complex process, and the introduction of "right" products to the market at the "right" time with minimized total costs becomes extremely challenging. Therefore, it is important for companies to understand the key concepts for successful innovation and new product development.

Because of its extreme importance to businesses, the topic of managing innovation processes and new product development projects has received significant attention in marketing, operations management and engineering design literature. See Krishnan and Ulrich (2001) for an excellent review of these literatures. In the meantime, it has become transparent that the nature of the topic requires a cross-functional approach with the use of multi-discipline tools. It is important that we develop an understanding of how different functional areas view the core issues and current challenges in innovation and product development, and construct theories, concepts and tools to contribute to effective managerial solutions in addressing these challenges. Contrasting views and complementary tools will contribute to a synergistic understanding of this truly cross-functional topic.

In this paper we will concentrate on the presentation of key operations management and marketing perspectives on the issues of effective innovation and new product development. The area encompasses a large number of topics; however, we will focus only on selected topics such as Platform-Based Product Development, Disruptive Innovation, Portfolio Management and Resource Allocation, and Incentives. We will present the most impactful research results and findings on the theory and practice of innovation and new product development, and also point out knowledge gaps that new research needs to fill.

2. Platform-Based Product Development

Today's market presents a great challenge in terms of meeting the needs of individual customers through high product variety. Offering high product variety is often very complex, and hence needs to be managed in the most efficient and effective way in order to remain competitive in the marketplace. One of the approaches considered by industrial firms to a successful family of products is the platform-based product development. A product platform, in its most general sense, can be defined as the collection of assets which are shared by individual products of a product family. These assets could be material assets such as components and processes, as well as intellectual assets such as knowledge, people and relationships (Robertson and Ulrich, 1998).

The use of platform-based product development provides several important benefits to companies in industrial practice, including the greater flexibility of tailoring products to meet the varying needs of different customer segments, reduction in system complexity, shorter product lead-times, reduction in unit production costs, and improved service levels and competitiveness within the marketplace (Robertson and Ulrich, 1998). Examples abound in practice. One of the most successful stories of product development using the platform-based approach is by Kodak in the development of its single-use cameras. In 1987, Fuji introduced the world's first single-use camera — the QuickSnap 35 mm — in the US market and it became an instant hit. Fuji's announcement of the single-use camera caught Kodak unprepared and brought its competitive, market and technical challenge into sharp focus. Kodak senior managers recognized that in order to create a successful, high-margin single-use camera to compete with Fuji, they needed to change the company's new product development process. Kodak's new strategy was to look at the development of a product family to better serve different customer segments using a common platform. Hence, from the very beginning, it designed its base product and its derivatives to share components and process steps. Kodak introduced its first model of the single-use camera almost a year later than the introduction of the QuickSnap, but by that time Fuji had already developed a second model, the QuickSnap Flash. However, because of its platform strategy, Kodak was able to develop the product derivatives much faster and more cheaply, and delivered twice as many products as Fuji, all of which became highly popular in the US market. As a consequence, the payback of the project was much faster than anticipated. Kodak captured more than 70% of the US single-use cameras market by late 1989 and had taken the market share back from Fuji (Clark and Wheelwright, 1993). Another example from a high-technology company, presented in Krishnan and Gupta (2001), illustrates the impact of platform-based development on unit production costs of individual products. The given example shows that the use of a common platform to develop two vertically differentiated products substantially decreases the unit production costs (30% for the high-end product and 20% for the low-end product) as a result of the larger volumes of various shared components. The fact that the fixed costs associated with the product development are less than 5% of the lifecycle gross profit of the product line makes the adoption of platform-based development much more profitable than the non-platform development.

There is an extensive literature on the design of product families, product platforms and their benefits. See Jiao *et al.* (2007) for an extensive review on the state-of-the-art in product family design and platform-based product development. However, platform-based product development may not be appropriate for some products and market conditions. One possible reason could be the considerably high fixed investment costs for developing product platforms which make the platform approach less profitable. There may also be other costs related to platforms that offset their benefits. For example, for some product types, the use of a common platform may result in the overdesign of low-end products or underdesign of high-end products due to the components shared across products (Krishnan and Gupta, 2001). If the overdesign costs are considerably higher, then adoption of independent (non-platform) product development can become more profitable than the platform approach. Another possible reason for the inappropriateness of product platforms could be the higher development time required for the initial product platform. For some industries, the development time for products may be the most important metric due to the potential loss of profits and market share to competitors from being late to market. Therefore, the early announcement of products could offset the benefits of platforms in this situation and make the independent product development more attractive for companies. In another context, the use of a common platform across the products may cause the firm to fail in differentiating its product or result in significantly higher costs for differentiation, hence making the platform approach less attractive (Robertson and Ulrich, 1998). Based on a study of one firm over a five-year period, Hauser (1999) also shows that the platform-based development approach does not always improve the profitability of a family of products.

The extant literature on platform-based product development discusses its benefits and possible disadvantages. The important question that we need to answer at this point is: for which product families and market conditions is the platform-based approach appropriate, and for which is it not? To the best of our knowledge, the work by Krishnan and Gupta (2001) is the first one that quantifies the trade-offs between the benefits of the platform-based approach and the certain additional costs imposed by its use; however, their analysis is quite limited. They only focus on the product types for which the platform approach results in the overdesign of low-end products, and explore the trade-offs between the overdesigned costs and platform scale economies. They analyze a stylized model to understand the appropriateness of using platform-based product development and its impact on the firm's product positioning decisions. They consider two vertically differentiated products that are offered to two market segments, namely, the low-end and high-end segments. They assume that the customers within a segment are homogeneous in the amount of utility they drive from a product, and that the high-end of the market is willing to pay more for a unit of performance level. They analyze four different approaches: (1) the platform-based approach for which the two products use a common platform and the platform constitutes the low-end product, (2) the independent (non-platform) development of two products, (3) the standardized product approach for which the firm offers a single standardized product for both segments, and (4) the niche product approach for which the firm offers a niche product and targets the high-end segment of the market.

They determine the regions of optimality for each one of these four approaches assuming negligibly small fixed development costs for the products when compared with the gross profits. Their results for the two-product approaches show that the platform-based development of products, when compared with the independent development, always leads to higher product differentiation and higher profit from the high-end product with an increase in its performance level. On the other hand, the profit from the low-end product, and hence the profitability of the platform approach, depends highly on the parameters which measure market diversity and platform and non-platform scale economies. The platform approach is not appropriate when market diversity is too low or too high or when non-platform scales are strong. The standardized product approach is optimal when market diversity is low or when there are significant non-platform scales, while the niche product approach is optimal when the market diversity is high, but not the non-platform scales. In the last part of their paper, Krishnan and Gupta (2001) also analyze the sequential introduction of products considering the introduction of the high-end product first and the low-end product second. Note that the low-end product cannot be introduced first due to the cannibalization from the high-end product. They argue that the higher product differentiation of the platform approach reduces the cannibalization of the high-end product by the low-end product; thus, the platform approach makes simultaneous introduction of products more attractive.

In their analysis, Krishnan and Gupta (2001) use a particular class of manufacturing cost functions that exhibit overdesign costs. Dana (2003) argues that the use of different types of cost functions for platform-based production in the presence of overdesign costs can reverse the results of Krishnan and Gupta (2001). For this purpose, he gives a general definition of overdesign costs associated with the platform production. Based on his definition, the cost savings for platform-based production increases as products become more differentiated and decreases as they become more similar. However, the cost function studied by Krishnan and Gupta (2001) does not satisfy Dana (2003)'s definition when platform scale economies exist. Using the class of cost functions he described, Dana (2003), as opposed to Krishnan and Gupta (2001), shows that the adoption of platform-based development results in lower product differentiation, and therefore simultaneous product introduction becomes less favorable to companies. In his study, Dana (2003) only looks at the case where it is optimal to produce both high- and low-quality products, but he does not compare the profits of the platform and non-platform approaches. Once products become less differentiated, then lower differentiation would probably drive the profits down and make the platform approach less attractive. Hence, it remains to check the optimal regions for platform and non-platform approaches as well as the single and two-product approaches using the overdesign costs defined by Dana (2003).

Both Krishnan and Gupta (2001) and Dana (2003) assume that the development costs are relatively small, and hence do not include them in their model. However, these costs could be significantly high for some industries, and may possibly impact firms' decisions on the use of product platforms. One possible extension of their work would be the consideration of development costs in the model. In addition, most companies have a limited budget allocated to their research and development activities. It would be interesting to see how a limited budget will change the firms' decisions.

Krishnan and Gupta (2001) study the single and two-product approaches in their work. Another interesting problem is to explore the impact of the platform approach on the optimal product line and product positioning decisions. Furthermore, the level of uncertainty in customer preferences and market size that exists at the product development stage can significantly affect the firms' decisions on the use of a common platform across the products, the choice of optimal product line and the optimal positioning of products. Once demand uncertainties are considered, then the platform approach will probably become more favorable due to the additional flexibility included into the system. Therefore, it is important to understand how the firms will benefit from platform-based production under demand uncertainties.

As practice shows, platform-based production is increasingly important for companies to sustain competitive advantage. In this context, the key element to success is determining the right time for the introduction of a new product platform as well as timing and positioning the core and derivative products associated with the new platform. Therefore, the area requires operations models to be developed, to find answers to the following questions: How should firms position their products on the same platform? How frequently should they launch the platform products? It is also important to understand the effect of limited resources on these decisions.

3. Disruptive Innovation

Disruptive innovation is one of the most important innovations that threatens the competitiveness and survival of many top companies in their industries. The concept of disruptive innovation was first introduced by Christensen (1997) with the concept of sustaining innovation. Sustaining innovation can be described as an incremental (or radical) increase in the performance and features of an existing product in an established market. Such innovation initially targets the high-end of the existing market to derive the best customers' higher margins, and then spreads downward through the low-end market segment over time. An example of a sustaining innovation would be the evolution of Pentium processors with new features added in every model which attract the high-end customers at first.

Disruptive innovation, on the other hand, is bringing a new product into the market which initially underperforms the existing product in the key dimensions that the high-end customers value, but is more appealing to low-end market or new customers on alternate dimensions such as its lower price, simplicity and more convenience of use. Disruptive innovation can be classified as "low-end disruptive innovation" or "new market disruptive innovation". Low-end disruptive innovation targets the less profitable customers in the low-end of the existing market who value price more than quality. Discount stores such as Wal-Mart and Target, which offer products at lower prices than department stores, are good examples of low-end disruption. New market disruptive innovation, on the other hand, opens up a new market by offering a new product in order to serve customers who have different needs than the existing customers, and who have not been previously served with the old products. Cell phones relative to landlines and hard disk drives with lower sizes are some examples of new market disruption, which we will discuss in more detail later in this section.

Disruptive innovation, initially, is not of any interest to the high-end market segment. However, over time, the increase in the performance of the new product along the dimensions that the high-end customers value is generally much higher than their increasing demands. Eventually, the new product replaces the old product starting from the low-end segment upward toward the high-end segment of the market. Most of the market's leading firms recognize the disruptive innovation in their industries, but they are often not willing to take advantage of it mainly because of the following reasons: (1) it is not appealing to the existing customers initially, or (2) they want to avoid cannibalization of sales of the existing product with a new one. Instead, they focus on successful sustaining innovations. However, Christensen's (1997) findings in his study of several industry examples show that even radical sustaining innovations by new entrants have rarely been a reason for the downfall of established firms, but it is the disruptive innovations that generally fail them. Hence, it is significantly important for the incumbents or the entrants to look for disruptive innovations and adopt these innovations. On top of this, it is also important for disruptive innovators to understand how their new product would enter the market and evolve over time.

Disruptive innovations and their impact on existing and emerging markets have been extensively discussed in literature by studying several examples from different industries (Christensen, 1997; Schmidt and Druehl, 2008). One classic example of disruptive innovation, which is typically studied in literature due to its complexity and dynamic nature, is from the hard disk drive industry. The disruptive innovations in the hard disk drive industry are the reductions in the sizes of the disk drives from 14-inch to 8-inch, 5.25-inch, 3.5-inch and to 2.5-inch and 1.8-inch. The 14-inch disk drives were produced to serve the mainframe computer market. When 8-inch drives were first developed by several new entrants with capacities of 10–40 MB, the mainframe market at the time was demanding drives with 300–400 MB capacity. Therefore, the new smaller disk drives were not of any interest to mainframe customers. However, the 8-inch drives opened up a new market, the minicomputer market, whose customers were more interested in low-priced, smaller size disk drives. After several sustaining innovations, the capacity of 8-inch drives increased considerably, and the firms producing 8-inch drives were able to meet the needs of the low-end mainframe market upward. Eventually, all the 14-inch manufacturers went out of the market. A similar pattern was observed for the reduction of the size of the disk drives from 8-inch to 5.25-inch, which opened up a new low-end market for desktop personal computers (see Christensen (1997) for a detailed explanation of all the phases).

Besides its extensive discussion, the analytical models developed to understand how disruptive innovations shape the market structure for old and new products over time are very limited. We now present the models analyzed in literature to explore the impact of disruptive innovations on the market outcomes (sales, prices and profits) of old and new products for different product characteristics and market conditions.

Schmidt and Porteus (2000) develop a model to understand the impact of a new product introduction on the existing market. They consider two differentiated products, new and old products, produced either by a single firm (monopoly) or by two firms competing for prices. Reservation price for a product (the sum of parth-worths for product's attributes) is assumed to be a linear function of the customer type, where customer type is described along one dimension and uniformly distributed over a specified range on that dimension. They assume that the slopes of the reservation price curves have the same sign. A customer buys the product with the highest positive surplus or buys nothing if both products have negative surpluses, where surplus is defined as the reservation price minus sales price. Each product is described only by its reservation price function and its unit production cost. Note that if the reservation price curve has a flatter slope, then the range of customers who value it similarly will be larger. Hence, the product is said to have a broader appeal if its slope is relatively flatter. Schmidt and Porteus (2000) study a single-period model (no improvement of products over time) and consider two ways that the new product can impact the market: the high-end encroachment and the low-end encroachment strategies. The term "encroachment" is used to describe the situation where the new product takes away sales from the old product. The high-end encroachment refers to the sustaining innovation and occurs when the new product attracts the high-end customers initially. The low-end encroachment, on the other hand, occurs when the new product attracts the low-end segment of the market first, possibly by opening up a new market (e.g., disruptive innovations). Schmidt and Porteus (2000) develop a measure of how superior (inferior) a product is to the other one, namely the degree of product/process innovation, with higher (lower) values representing superior (inferior) innovation. The degree of innovation for a product depends on all the parameters of the model. While it increases with the difference between its maximum reservation price and its unit production cost and decreases with the slope of its reservation price curve, the impact of the parameters for the other product is in the opposite direction.

Schmidt and Porteus (2000) determine the regions for the market positioning of the two products for a given level of degree of product/process innovation. Under competition, the market outcome ranges from monopoly for the old product, to constrained monopoly for the old product (i.e., the product has all the sales but its price is constrained by the competitor), differentiated duopoly, constrained monopoly for the new product and monopoly for the new product, as the innovation represented by the new product ranges from drastically inferior (lowest values for the degree of innovation) to drastic innovation (highest values for the degree of innovation). Similarly, for the monopoly case, the possible market outcomes would be monopoly for the old product (low values for the degree of innovation), joint monopoly (intermediate values for the degree of innovation), or monopoly for the new product (high values for the degree of innovation). For a given set of model parameters that describe the products, Schmidt and Porteus (2000) show that the region for the differentiated duopoly under competitive setting enlarges the one for the joint monopoly. To summarize, the way a new product impacts the market structure depends significantly on: (1) who offers the new product (the incumbent or a new entrant), (2) the difference between its maximum reservation price and its unit production cost, and (3) the relative appeal of the product (broad or niche). In the last part of their work, the authors carry out a numerical study to gain insights into some of the market outcomes of product innovations such as Pentium microprocessors (high-end encroachment) and disk drive industry (low-end encroachment).

Schmidt and Druehl (2005) extend the work of Schmidt and Porteus (2000) to include the dynamic evolution of the two products offered in the market. They assume that performance of the product in the dimensions of quality, customers' preferences, reservation prices and unit production costs changes over time. They incorporate these assumptions into their model by considering the intercept and slope of reservation price curves and the unit production costs as functions of time. At each point of time, they myopically determine the market outcomes for the products as in Schmidt and Porteus (2000), by only considering the reservation price curves and production costs at that point. For their analysis they define two terms: depth ratio and breadth factor. Depth ratio is defined as the ratio of the new product's depth to the old product's depth, where the depth of a product is described as the difference between its maximum possible reservation price (i.e., intercept of the reservation price curve) and its unit production cost. In other words, depth represents the maximum possible profit margin for a unit of product. Breadth factor is related to the slopes of the reservation price curves, and describes the extent to which the new product becomes relatively more broadly attractive over time. Schmidt and Druehl (2005) show that the ratio of the market shares for the differentiated duopoly or joint monopoly can be fully determined by the depth ratio and breadth factor. Their model suggests that relative improvements in performance and in costs over time are required for a product to achieve a superior market share.

To understand how a new product's depth (old product's depth assumed to be constant over time) and breadth change over time, Schmidt and Druehl (2005) discuss two specifications for changes in depth ratio and breadth factor. They assume that the changes are either linear in time or follow an S-curve pattern (logistic function) for which the increase is slow initially, then speeds up and slows down after maturity. They apply their model to test linear and logistic models using the empirical data from the hard disk drive and microprocessor industries. They show that the logistic model has a better fit in both industries, but the fit is much better than the linear model for the disk drive industry.

Druehl and Schmidt (2008) extend the works of Schmidt and Porteus (2000) and Schmidt and Druehl (2005) by considering a different low-end encroachment strategy which starts with opening up a new market. Their strategy is different than the one studied in previous works in terms of the type of market opened up initially for the new product. The previous works assume that, before the new product starts encroaching from the low-end segment upward, it opens up a new market on the low-end fringe of the established market, i.e., the needs of customers in the new market are incrementally different from the ones who are in the low-end segment of the existing market (hard disk drive example). Druehl and Schmidt (2008) name this strategy as "fringe-market low-end encroachment". However, in their paper, they assume that the new product first opens up a "detached" market in which the needs of the customers are drastically different from the ones in the low-end of the existing market. They call this strategy "detached-market low-end encroachment". An example of a disruptive innovation with a detached market strategy is the cell phone innovation. The first cell phones were sold at around $4,000 and initially attracted customers with a strong need for mobility such as a construction foreman. Hence, the cell phones first opened up a detached market whose customers were willing to pay higher prices for mobility. For the customers of landlines, coverage and perception were much more important. As the cell phone's performance on coverage and perception improves, it begins to encroach from the low-end segment of the market for landlines upward.

Whether the low-end encroachment strategy opens up a fringe or detached market depends on the slopes of products' reservation price curves. If the slopes have the same sign, then the new product, which initially is offered at a lower price, opens up a fringe market (Schmidt and Porteus, 2000). However, if the slopes have opposite signs, then the new product, which initially is offered at a higher price, opens up a detached market as in the study of Druehl and Schmidt (2008).

Druehl and Schmidt (2008) analyze the detached market strategy, focusing particularly on the cell phone example. They assume that the new product (cell phone) is a better substitute for the old product (landline), hence the slope of its reservation price curve is more flat. Their analysis at a given time point leads to the following conclusions for competitive firms: (1) if both product depths (maximum possible profit margins) are low, then the market outcome would be detached monopolies where each firm sells its product in a separated market with a monopoly price; (2) if one of the products has a sufficiently higher depth, then the outcome would be a constrained monopoly for that product where it will serve the entire market at a constrained price which is lower than the monopoly price; (3) if both product depths are relatively large, then the outcome would be a differentiated duopoly where the firms split the market. The differentiated duopoly can come out in two different ways depending on the value of the surplus for the customer type who is indifferent between buying one product versus the other (i.e., surplus at the point that splits the two markets). A positive surplus implies that each firm will have higher sales if not constrained by the rival's decisions; hence the competition is more aggressive for the customers in the middle for this case. In the case of a zero surplus, however, the market presence of the competitor does not have a significant impact on the firm's profitability; hence the competition is somewhat mild for middle segments. The authors' analysis of the monopoly setting shows that the conditions for a joint detached monopoly where each product serves one end of the potential market are exactly the same for the joint monopolies of the competitive case. On the other hand, if the depth of one of the products is significantly higher, then that product will cover the entire market offering the price equal to its minimum reservation price. If both depths are relatively large, then the outcome would be a joint covered market; the products cover the entire market, and each product will have a positive sale with a price above its monopoly price. Results show that if the new product is initially poor in traditional dimensions, but superior in alternate dimensions, then the product innovation is attractive even to the incumbent. The incumbent can take advantage of product innovation, by targeting the new product to the other end of the potential market and deriving higher surpluses from customers. Druehl and Schmidt (2008) apply their model to understand the progress of cell phones over time relative to landlines using the best-fit logistic model for the changes in depth ratio and breadth factor based on the empirical data for landlines and cell phones.

All the models we discussed in this section assume that the initial product characteristics such as its performance and unit production cost are given. However, the positioning of new products is one of the most important problems that firms face in product innovation. Therefore, models that incorporate the optimal positioning of a new product, which will also determine its optimal encroachment strategy, are required. On the other hand, optimal investment decisions for product development at a given time point are mostly limited by the budget available. In this case, firms need to make decisions on how to allocate their limited budget to product development opportunities. Models need to be developed to understand the evolution of products over time depending on the budget available at each time point.

4. Portfolio Management and Resource Allocation

One other important aspect of new product development that profoundly impacts the success and competitiveness of a company is effective project selection and allocation of limited resources (e.g., budget, labor, and machines) among these projects. Choosing the right projects when resources are limited is a very challenging and complex problem; hence, in order to handle this problem, companies require a systematic portfolio management which effectively guides their project selection and resource allocation decisions. Portfolio management in NPD is a dynamic decision-making process, where the existing and new product development projects are revised in a timely manner. The projects are evaluated, selected and prioritized, and available resources are allocated among the projects. The evidence shows that superior portfolio management is one of the most important aspects of the best performing companies in NPD; yet very few businesses have a systematic portfolio management in place (Cooper and Edgett, 2006).

There are many reasons why companies have problems managing their portfolio of projects in an effective way. One of the main reasons for many companies is that they consider each individual project in isolation. This approach leads to ineffectual use of available resources and results in suboptimal solutions. For a better management of an NPD project portfolio, companies must view the set and mix of projects together, consider the interdependencies between them, and focus on the optimal allocation ofresources among the projects. In other words, companies need an aggregate project plan to improve the management of NPD projects (see Wheelwright and Clark (1992) for a list of eight steps of an aggregate project plan).

Another reason why many companies cannot successfully manage their portfolio of projects is that they have far too many projects going on at once, resulting in unanticipated consequences, such as under-resourced projects, overflowing investments, an increase in the development time of projects, or failure of some of the projects (Cooper and Edgett, 2001, 2006; Wheelwright and Clark, 1992). Hence, it is important for companies to maintain the right number of projects for their limited resources by focusing on the projects that are of higher value and that are in line with their development strategies in order to maximize the value of their portfolio.

One other reason for a poor portfolio management is companies' greater focus on incremental development projects, which are characterized by improvements and modifications to existing company products. These are short-term projects with lower risk and quick returns, but they generate only incremental revenue and profit. According to an APQC 2004 study cited in Cooper (2005), the percentage of incremental development projects significantly increased (80%) from 1990 to 2004, while the percentage of new-to-world innovations and new product lines to companies significantly decreased (44% and 30%, respectively). The study also reveals that while the worst performing firms are highly focused on incremental projects, the best performers have a diverse set of projects including the new-to-world, new product lines, existing product lines and incremental projects. This fact underscores the importance of achieving a right balance of projects within the portfolio in terms of long-term vs. short-term projects; or high-risk vs. low-risk projects; and across various markets, technologies, product categories, and project types (Cooper and Edgett, 2001).

To visualize a portfolio's balance across various product offerings and project types, Wheelwright and Clark (1992) present an effective way of categorizing different types of NPD projects using a bubble diagram. The diagram displays the projects in two dimensions as bubbles, where the size of bubbles denotes the resources required. The authors define the two dimensions as degree of change in the product and degree of change in the manufacturing process. As the degree of change in any one of these dimensions becomes larger, the risk associated with the project as well as the resources required increases. Wheelwright and Clark (1992) characterize five categories of NPD projects, three of which are defined as commercial development projects, namely derivative, breakthrough and platform projects. Derivative projects involve incremental product changes only (e.g., a new feature) or incremental process changes only (e.g., improved reliability) or incremental changes in both dimensions. On the other hand, breakthrough projects involve major changes in both dimensions and bring new products and processes to the market or to the world. Platform projects lie in the middle of the derivative and breakthrough projects, and offer fundamental improvements over previous generations of products across a range of performance attributes such as cost, quality, size, speed, etc. Note that the projects that involve major changes in one dimension but incremental changes into the other dimension do not fall into any of these categories. These projects are not breakthrough projects and yet require extensive resources; hence they are of low value to the company and can be abandoned for the company's advantage when resources are scarce. The other two categories are research and development projects which are a precursor to product/process development, and alliances and partnerships which can be either basic research or product/process development. This type of classification can be used to identify gaps (room for improvement) that exist in the development strategy and to help firms make more informed decisions regarding the execution of the right balance of development projects and the allocation of available resources among them (Cooper and Edgett, 2001).

As mentioned previously, maintaining a diverse, balanced project portfolio is a key to success in NPD. However, companies should be aware of the fact that different projects involve different levels of uncertainty and risk, and hence require a different management approach. Based on a study of 16 projects in several business areas, De Meyer *et al.* (2002) show that managers consistently fail to recognize different types of uncertainties associated with different projects, and therefore fail to manage them in the right way. As a matter of fact, the projects end up with an overrun schedule, overflowing budget, compromised specifications, or else the project just dies. In their study, De Meyer *et al.* (2002) classify the uncertainties into four categories — variation, foreseen uncertainty, unforeseen uncertainty, and chaos — and talk about the approaches to manage each uncertainty. As the project ranges from incremental changes to radical innovations, the uncertainty associated with it ranges from variation to chaos. Variation comes from combined small influences. Projects that are characterized by variation have clearly defined objectives and follow a predictable route, but schedules and budgets may vary from their projected values. Managers can easily manage this uncertainty by leaving a small portion of resources uncommitted to deal with any variations. Foreseen uncertainty is not only identifiable, but it is also understood influences that may or may not occur. To manage foreseen uncertainty, managers create contingency plans to handle the possible events that could affect the project. Unforeseen uncertainty involves major factors that cannot be predicted during project planning or are considered as unlikely; hence there is no contingency plan. For this case of uncertainty, the project team should continually scan for emerging influences and must solve new problems every time new information arises. For the projects characterized by chaos, even the basic structure of the plan is uncertain. Often the final results are completely different from what was initially intended. This uncertainty requires greater flexibility and creativity in the acquisition of resources and competencies, which would allow the managers to repeatedly and completely redefine the project.

After reviewing the important issues related to effective project portfolio management in NPD, we will now focus on the problem of optimal portfolio selection. The NPD portfolio selection problem is very difficult due to the considerations of its dynamic nature, scarcity of resources, strategic alignment, project interdependencies, and outcome uncertainties (Kavadias and Chao, 2008). Many approaches have been developed in practice and literature to model the portfolio selection problem. The popular models used in practice for portfolio decisions are scoring models. These models use a set of criteria defined by management (e.g., strategic alignment, product advantage, market attractiveness, synergies, technical feasibility and risk versus return) and score each project based on the selected criteria. The criteria scores are then summarized into an overall score for each project (e.g., weighted averages of criteria scores), and finally the best projects are chosen until resources run out (Cooper and Edgett, 2001). These models are widely used in practice because they are easy to implement and can incorporate multiple criteria important to businesses. However, they come up short in incorporating uncertainty or interactions among projects, and are unable to optimize the mix of projects.

The models that optimally select the project portfolio are based on mathematical programming approaches. The most important facet of these models is their capability of incorporating possible interactions among the projects such as the effect of sharing the same resources, complementarity and substitution effects, and the effect of one project on the probability of success of another one (Schmidt, 1993; Loch *et al.*, 2001; Dickinson *et al.*, 2001). These early models assume that the projects are either fully implemented or not implemented; hence the formulation of the models takes the form of knapsack problem which is difficult to solve. Furthermore, the models are not robust to changes in parameters; hence they require accurate data which is unavailable in most cases. As a matter of fact, these models have not found widespread acceptance in practice (see Eilat *et al.* (2006) and references therein). In a recent study, Beaujon *et al.* (2001) consider the case where partial funding and implementation of projects (in the sense of implementing them at a slower pace) are allowed. This assumption significantly reduces the complexity of the problem to be solved since it is no longer a combinatorial optimization problem. Beaujon *et al.* (2001) formulated the model as a linear programming problem that can easily be solved for a given data set. Another powerful feature of this model as shown by Beaujon *et al.* (2001) is that the solution is reasonably robust to rather large variation in the measure of the portfolio value (e.g., Net Present Value).

Loch and Kavadias (2002) developed a dynamic programming model of portfolio selection at the R&D program level focusing on investments in product lines. Similar to Beaujon *et al.* (2001), they assume that the investment in a product line is not an all-or-nothing decision but can be continuously adjusted. Their model is one of the most comprehensive models studied in literature, and provides general managerial insights for the project portfolio selection and resource allocation decisions in NPD. The model considers multiple periods and multiple product lines. It takes into account uncertain market payoffs, and decreasing or increasing returns from NPD investments. The uncertain market payoffs are included in the system by considering the maximum possible profits that the firm may possibly earn from a given market segment (i.e., potential market profit) during a given time period as a random variable. The fraction of the expected potential profit that a product line can achieve is represented by a return function which accounts for both current investments and the carryover investments from previous periods. The model also incorporates market interactions through complementarity or substitutability effects, and management risk aversion.

Loch and Kavadias (2002) present closed form solutions for the characterization of optimal budget allocation policy when there are two product lines and two decision time periods, but state that their key result also holds for multiple product lines and multiple periods. When investments on product lines have increasing returns (convex return function), they show that at each period it is optimal to allocate the total budget to the product line with the highest expected return. However, when investments have decreasing returns (concave return function), then it is optimal to split the available budget at each period among the product lines according to their total marginal benefits (current and carried over to the subsequent periods), i.e., the next dollar should be invested to the product line which has the highest total marginal benefits (key result of their paper). In their paper, they also explore the impact of model parameters, such as marginal investment returns, investment carryover effects and expected potential market payoffs, on optimal investments when the budgets are split.

In a different study, Kavadias and Loch (2003) study the resource allocation problem at the project level. They develop a dynamic prioritization policy to optimally allocate a scarce resource among ongoing NPD projects, where the resource can only work on one project at a time (e.g., testing lab, specialized engineer). The delay of a project incurs a cost (cost of delaying the introduction of the product) which is defined as an increasing fraction of the expected potential final payoff which is independent of the performance state of the project. The discrete time performance state transitions are assumed to be Markovian with known probabilities. For example, if the project goes as planned, then its performance state does not change. Kavadias and Loch (2003) did not consider the discount rate in their model, since the duration of a project at a scarce resource is generally very short when compared with its total duration. They further assume that the projects are not abandoned based on their performance state during their process at the scarce resource. Their results for the analysis of two projects show that at each review period, the scarce resource is allocated to the project that has the highest expected delay loss, which is calculated as if it started after the other project is completely finished without interruptions at the scarce resource. If there are more than two projects, then in each review period it is optimal to allocate the scarce resource to the project that has the higher expected delay loss when compared with any of the other projects. However, Kavadias and Loch (2003) show that when the delay losses are non-linear, then it may not be possible to find an optimal ordering, i.e., it is possible to have circular delay cost comparisons. Optimal ordering of projects is guaranteed only when delay costs are linear.

As mentioned above, different projects have different risk and uncertainty levels and require different management processes. While radical breakthrough projects face higher risks and uncertainties, the ones associated with incremental/derivative projects are lower. It is clear that firms should invest in the development of both breakthrough projects and incremental projects in order to remain competitive in the market. Therefore, it is important for firms to understand how to deal with different types of projects, and how to allocate available resources among these projects. Current operations management research mainly focuses on short-term benefits of resource allocation; hence, it either deals with incremental projects, or the results derived from the existing models suggest an incremental strategy. However, the models are required to incorporate firms' long-term benefits also for more efficient resource allocation decisions. One other important point that the current research on resource allocation does not take into account is the impact of competition on optimal allocation of limited resources to the development of different projects. The competitors' actions during the development process can increase the importance of some of the projects, and hence can affect the firm's resource allocation decisions.

5. Incentives

In today's competitive market, companies are under increasing pressure to reduce the cost and cycle time of introducing new products. While reducing time-to-market is a key success factor, speeding products to the market may lead to negative consequences, such as project cancellation, reduced profitability, and most importantly the managers' increasing focus on the incremental improvements of existing products, which significantly reduces the long-run success and competitiveness of companies. One effective way of introducing new products to the market in a timely and cost-effective manner is through the successful management of the human resources (e.g., managers, engineers) in NPD projects. Successful human resource management can be achieved by using proper incentive schemes to motivate the managers and engineers who are responsible for the development process. However, the study of incentives and their impact on innovation and product development has been largely ignored by researchers. Only a few recent papers study this aspect of NPD by using principal-agent models.

In a recent study, Chao *et al.* (2009) investigate the impact of funding authority and incentives on the dynamic allocation of resources between different NPD projects over a specified portfolio review cycle. They consider two types of development projects: a relatively incremental project that focuses on improvement of an existing product, and a more radical project that focuses on development of a new product. They study a two-stage model and formulate it as a principal-agent model. In the first stage, the senior management (principal) chooses the funding authority. The authors consider two forms of funding authority, namely fixed funding and variable funding. The fixed funding is set by the senior management, while the variable funding is defined as the percentage of revenue derived from the existing product. While the manager (agent) does not have authority over funding when it is fixed, she has the authority to use the revenue derived from existing product sales to fund NPD efforts when funding is variable. In the second stage, the principal offers a linear wage contract to the agent under noisy information signals he receives regarding her allocation of resources. The offered wage contract consists of a fixed part plus incentives that depend on the agent's efforts over the portfolio review cycle. The senior management determines the incentives for the manager's NPD efforts in a way that maximizes his expected payoffs. At this stage, the manager makes the resource allocation decisions between the NPD projects in such a way that maximizes her expected payoff that consists of explicit wage incentives and implicit career concerns. The manager's career concerns are affected by her use of the designated budget. While a budget overrun implies mismanagement of resources and has a negative career concerns effect, a budget surplus implies skillful resource management and has a positive career concerns effect.

The results of Chao *et al.* (2009) show that managers have higher incentives for their NPD efforts when they are given funding authority; hence their investments in both improvement of the existing product and new product development are higher, and result in a higher joint surplus. However, the NPD portfolio balance shifts towards improvement of the existing product when compared with fixed funding, which can negatively affect the company's success in the long run. It is reasonable for the manager to be more inclined towards an incremental development strategy under variable funding, since she uses the revenue derived from the existing product to fund both projects. Furthermore, as the agent's career concerns become more significant, her investment efforts for the two projects decrease under both funding authorities. The only exception is that, the agent's efforts to improve the existing product will be higher in the early periods (i.e., more incremental strategy in the early periods) under variable funding in order to generate more revenues from the existing product in later periods to reduce the risks associated with her career advancement. Thus, the agent's increased career concerns reduce the explicit wage incentives, as well as the joint surplus, and shift the NPD portfolio balance towards a more incremental strategy.

In another recent study, Mihm (2009) explores the impact of incentives on NPD project outcomes and development times in a game theoretic setting. In this study he focuses on the development of a new product that consists of N components, each designed by one engineer or a small team of engineers. Each component provides a utility to the firm which depends on the component's development cost (i.e., utility increases with the cost but at a decreasing rate), and a parameter which captures the cost-performance trade-offs associated with the component and which is private knowledge to the engineer. A smaller value for this cost-performance trade-off parameter implies that it is more costly to increase the value of the component. Assuming that the components are independent, the overall utility of the component to the firm is defined as the sum of individual component utilities. At the end of the development process, the firm introduces the product if it has a positive value to the firm, or otherwise cancels the project. The model assumes that each component's utility to the engineer can be different from its utility to the firm, i.e., engineers may be willing to design a more sophisticated component than what the firm desires. This utility difference between the engineer and the firm is captured by a parameter which is called the firm's cost compliance culture. While a high cost compliance culture implies similar component utilities for the two parties, a low value implies the engineer's higher willingness to overspend. Mihm (2009) models the development process as a two-stage game, with each stage referring to a different phase of the project development process. In the first stage each engineer defines the cost for the design of his component, and in the second stage he revises his decision and may lower his cost. The level of utility each engineer receives depends on the engineer's cost decisions made at the second stage.

In the first part of his study, Mihm (2009) discusses the existing NPD project management approaches. In the traditional approach, the engineers announce their cost decisions at the first stage and then observe the others' decisions. If at this stage the project faces cancellation, then the engineers revise their decisions in the second stage to avoid this undesirable result. This approach actually reduces the firm's profit unless the cost compliance culture is strong (i.e., high alignment between the goals of engineers and those of the firm), and will most likely result in late design changes due to cost gaming, leading to an increased product development time. Companies that have weak cost compliance cultures can improve their profits by following a heavyweight project management approach. In this approach, the manager inspects some percentage of the engineers' work at each stage after they have announced their cost decisions. During the inspection process the manager learns about the component and the type of engineer, and adjusts the engineer's cost decision to one that is optimal for the firm. However, it is not practical for the manager to inspect all the engineers. In his paper, Mihm (2009) determines a range for inspection and cost levels such that the heavyweight project management approach results in better outcomes when compared with the traditional approach; however, given the high inspection costs and the manager's low inspection capacity, the heavyweight project management approach is neither affordable nor practical for firms.

Mihm (2009) shows that providing specifically designed individual incentives can eliminate the problems inherent in the existing project management approaches. When individual incentives are considered by the firm, then the engineers and the firm should agree on a contract with incentives at the very beginning. The provided incentives should aim to align the goals of the firm with the goals of the engineers. Individual incentives studied by Mihm (2009) include Bayesian mechanisms, profit sharing, and component-level target costing. With Bayesian mechanisms, the firm defines a transfer function to optimize the trade-off between the costs of the incentives and the benefits gained through engineers' improved behavior. The use of Bayesian mechanisms may improve the profitability of the firm and project timing when compared to the traditional management approach. Furthermore, this incentive scheme is affordable even for large development projects. However, it is not practical since it requires extensive information about engineers' type distributions and the transfer function is highly non-linear. On the other hand, providing incentives using profit sharing and cost targets is more simple and practical. While a profit sharing contract gives bonuses to engineers when the profit exceeds some threshold level, where the bonus is defined as some percentage of the positive surplus (linear contracts), the cost targeting contract penalizes engineers if they exceed the component target costs set by the firm. Mihm (2009) shows that, as in Bayesian mechanisms, profit sharing and cost targeting contracts can improve on the existing management approaches by avoiding cost gaming iterations without contradicting engineers' self-interests, and can also help reduce the product development times. Furthermore, a linear profit sharing contract is shown to improve the project outcomes as well if the project creates a high enough benefit for engineers. While a profit sharing incentive scheme can be effectively used for small projects, it may not be affordable for large projects since it will compel the firm to share a large portion of its profits with the engineers unless the project has a very high value. On the other hand, cost targeting contracts will provide higher profits than the traditional approach as the firm has more accurate knowledge about the component, and they can even be affordable for large development projects. To conclude, we can say that, if the cost compliance culture of the firm is weak, then existing project management approaches can be complemented with the appropriate explicit incentive schemes described by Mihm (2009).

The study by Chao *et al.* (2009) shows that giving funding authority to the managers who make the resource allocation decisions as well as their increased career concerns shift the balance of the NPD portfolio towards a more incremental strategy, i.e., the managers' interest is in investing in improvements to existing products. While this provides higher profits in the short run, it will affect the firms' long-run success and competitiveness in a negative way. One possible future research direction is to develop proper incentive schemes that increase the managers' willingness to allocate more resources to radical breakthrough projects, and hence shift the portfolio balance towards a radical strategy.

6. Putting the Framework into Practice

With quickly changing customer tastes and shortened product lifecycles, organizations nowadays are under constant pressure of introducing new products to the market. Many organizations have multiple product and process development projects going at the same time with limited resources dedicated to these projects. Practice shows that carrying out too many projects at once adversely affects the successful completion of each project. Hence, it is critical for organizations to focus on the right number of projects based on available resources. It is also important for organizations to choose the right mix of projects that will provide the greatest value.

The projects can range from incremental changes to existing products to radical or breakthrough projects. While the incremental projects have low levels of uncertainty and risk with little impact on the growth of companies, the outcome of radical projects is highly uncertain and unpredictable, but has the greatest impact on the competitive position of the companies. Therefore, it is important for companies to find the optimal balance between different types of projects. Evidence shows that the leading companies in industry have a diverse and balanced project portfolio. It is also important for companies to understand the uncertainties and risks associated with each project selected, and to find the most effective way of managing these projects.

Once the organizations select their development projects, they have to make decisions on the allocation of available resources among them. As shown by Loch and Kavadias (2002), the allocation of resources among the projects highly depends on the expected returns from the projects. If the investments have increasing returns, then at each period it is optimal to focus on the projects with the highest expected returns. However, if the investments have decreasing returns, then it is optimal to split the resources between different projects based on their marginal benefits.

Effective allocation of resources would significantly improve the profitability of organizations. On the other hand, the career concerns of managers could affect their product development efforts to the disadvantage of the company. The managers could be more willing to invest in incremental projects when they have high career concerns, which would negatively affect the company's future success and profitability. Therefore, the use of proper incentives to motivate the managers is important for the long-run success and profitability of the company. As discussed in Mihm (2009), specifically designed individual incentives can help align the goals of the managers with those of the firm. Therefore, incentives provided to managers will not only increase the firm's profitability, but will also help reduce product development times which is extremely important for companies facing the pressures of shortened product lifecycles and increased market competition.

To summarize, this chapter discusses the emerging opportunities and challenges for firms in innovation and new product development, and develops an understanding of theories, concepts and tools that contribute to effective managerial solutions in addressing these challenges. We discuss some of the major key factors associated with the successful new product development initiatives and present strategies for the effective management of new product and process development efforts. We hope that the review will help managers understand the key concepts in new product development.

7. Conclusion

In today's rapidly changing market, introducing new products on a continuous basis is highly important to the success and competitive position of many organizations. The process of bringing successful new products to the market in a timely and cost-effective manner, while providing good value for customers, is a big challenge for most organizations. In this chapter, we discuss some of the important challenges that organizations face during the product development process, focusing on the selected topics of platform-based product development, disruptive innovation, portfolio management and resource allocation, and incentives. We provide a brief review of the existing literature on effective management of new product and process development efforts, and present the most impactful research results and findings from the study of quantitative models to important business problems.

As noted throughout the chapter, there is an extensive qualitative discussion in the literature on managing new product and process development. However, the research being pursued with the use of operations models is quite limited, and hence provides many challenges and opportunities to researchers. We present the current knowledge gaps and possible opportunities for new research directions at the end of each section. One major weakness of almost all the models presented in this chapter that is worth mentioning again is that they do not capture the uncertainties associated with the product and process development activities. The fact that there are high uncertainties in customer preferences, market size and market payoffs in the development stage requires more advanced models to be developed. Operations models that incorporate various uncertainties would offer more valuable insight to organizations on the impact of these uncertainties on strategic development decisions, such as product line design and allocation of available resources. Furthermore, models are also required to jointly optimize these decisions.

References

Beaujon, G. J., S. P. Marin, and G. C. McDonald (2001). Balancing and Optimizing a Portfolio of R&D Projects. *Naval Research Logistics*, 48(1): 18–40.

Chao, R. O., S. Kavadias, and C. Gaimon (2009). Revenue-Driven Resource Allocation: Funding Authority, Incentives, and New Product Development Portfolio Management. *Management Sci.*, 55(9): 1556–1569.

Christensen, C. M. (1997). *The Innovator's Dilemma.* Harvard Business School Press, Boston, MA.

Clark, K. and S. Wheelwright (1993). *Managing Product and Process Development.* The Free Press, New York, NY.

Cooper, R. G. (2005). Your NPD Portfolio May Be Harmful to Your Business's Health. PDMA Visions, XXIX, 3 (April), 22–26.

Cooper, R. G. and S. J. Edgett (2001). Portfolio Management for New Products "Picking the Winners". Working Paper No. 11, Product Development Institute.

Cooper, R. G. and S. J. Edgett (2006). Ten Ways to Make Better Portfolio and Project Selection Decisions. PDMA Visions, XXX, 3 (June), 11–15.

Dana, J. (2003). Remark on Appropriateness and Impact of Platform-Based Product Development. *Management Sci.*, 49(9): 1264–1267.

De Meyer, A., C. H. Loch, and M. T. Pich (2002). Managing Project Uncertainty: From Variation to Chaos. *MIT Sloan Management Review*, 43(2): 60–67.

Dickinson, M. W., A. C. Thornton, and S. Graves (2001). Technology Portfolio Management: Optimizing Interdependent Projects over Multiple Time Periods. *IEEE Trans. Engrg. Management*, 48(4): 518–527.

Druehl, C. T. and G. M. Schmidt (2008). A Strategy for Opening a New Market and Encroaching on the Lower End of the Existing Market. *Production and Oper. Management*, 17(1): 44–60.

Eilat, H., B. Golany, and A. Shtub (2006). Constructing and Evaluating Balanced Portfolios of R&D Projects with Interactions: A DEA-Based Methodology. *Eur. J. Oper. Research*, 172(3): 1018–1039.

Hauser, J. H. (1999). Strategic Priorities in Product Development. Working Paper, MIT Sloan School, Cambridge, MA.

Jiao, J., T. W. Simpson, and Z. Siddique (2007). Product Family Design and Platform-Based Product Development: A State-of-the-Art Review. *J. Intell. Manuf.*, 18: 5–29.

Kavadias, S. and C. H. Loch (2003). Optimal Project Sequencing with Recourse at a Scarce Resource. *Production and Oper. Management*, 12(4): 433–444.

Kavadias, S. and R. O. Chao (2008). Resource Allocation and New Product Development. In C. H. Loch and S. Kavadias (eds.), *Handbook of New Product Development Management*. Elsevier/Butterworth-Heinemann, Oxford, UK, 135–163.

Krishnan, V. and K. T. Ulrich (2001). Product Development Decisions: A Review of Literature. *Management Sci.*, 47(1): 1–21.

Krishnan, V. and S. Gupta (2001). Appropriateness and Impact of Platform-Based Product Development. *Management Sci.*, 47(1): 52–68.

Loch, C. H., M. T. Pich, C. Terwiesch, and M. Urbschat (2001). Selecting R&D Projects at BMW: A Case Study of Adopting Mathematical Programming Models. *IEEE Trans. Engrg. Management*, 48(1): 70–80.

Loch, C. H. and S. Kavadias (2002). Dynamic Portfolio Selection of NPD Programs Using Marginal Returns. *Management Sci.*, 48(10): 1227–1241.

Mihm, J. (2009). Incentives in New Product Development Projects and the Role of Target Costing. Working Paper, INSEAD, France.

Robertson, D. and K. Ulrich (1998). Planning for Product Platforms. *Sloan Management Review*, 39(4): 19–31.

Schmidt, R. L. (1993). A Model for R&D Project Selection with Combined Benefit, Outcome and Resource Interactions. *IEEE Trans. Engrg. Management*, 40(4): 403–410.

Schmidt, G. M. and C. T. Druehl (2005). Changes in Product Attributes and Costs as Divers of New Product Diffusion and Substitution. *Production and Oper. Management*, 14(3): 272–285.

Schmidt, G. M. and C. T. Druehl (2008). When is a Disruptive Innovation Disruptive? *J. Product Innovation Management*, 25: 347–369.

Schmidt, G. M. and E. L. Porteus (2000). The Impact of an Integrated Marketing and Manufacturing Innovation. *Manufacturing and Ser. Oper. Management*, 2(4): 317–336.

Wheelwright, S. C. and K. B. Clark (1992). Creating Project Plans to Focus Product Development. *Harvard Business Review*, 70(2): 70–82.

Chapter 4

Innovation and Finance:
A Survey

Anjan V. Thakor

*John E. Simon Professor of Finance and Director of the WFA Center
for Finance and Accounting Research and Doctoral Program,
Olin Business School, Washington University in St. Louis*

This paper reviews two strands of research-based literature on innovation. The first strand deals with the financial valuation implications of innovations. It addresses questions related to how innovation is financed and its impact on the shareholder value of the firm that is engaging in that innovation. The second strand of the literature deals with financial innovation, namely the process by which new financial securities and structures are created. The focus of the survey is on understanding the underlying economic forces related to innovation and the managerial decision-making implications of these forces.

1. Introduction

The purpose of this review paper is to present a survey of the research on innovation from a financial economics perspective. There is an extensive body of high-quality academic and applied research on this subject, and the goal here is to provide a synthesis of this work, with an eye toward the key insights that have emerged thus far and the open questions that still remain as important challenges for future research.

From a financial economics perspective, the research on innovation can be broadly classified into two groups: (1) the valuation implications of innovation in general, and how Finance links innovation to shareholder value, as well as what Finance research teaches us about the interaction between innovation and the manner in which this innovation is financed; and (2) financial innovation, including the incentives for financial innovation, the identity of innovators, and the social welfare implications of financial innovation.

The research papers that deal with these two strands of literature fall into two distinct camps, with differences in focus as well as in research methodologies. My goal will be to orient the discussion toward the underlying economics as well as the managerial decision-making connotations, rather than on the research methodologies.

There is no question that innovation is a key element of economic growth. Some of the most spectacular bursts of economic activity have occurred as a result of technological and other forms of innovation. Recall the economic transitions that took us from buggy whips to automobiles, from ocean ships to airplanes, from star gazing to space travel, from mainframe computers to hand-held computing devices, and so on. Each of these innovations led to quantum leaps in economic activity and wealth. Each led to a host of "subsidiary innovations" that were often unpredictable at the outset, but made significant contributions to economic growth.

Thus, it is not difficult to make a strong case for an improved understanding of innovation as a *process*. And it is a process. Although many think of innovation as the outcome of creative genius — and there is no denying that creative genius plays an important role — the fact is that innovation success often depends on a host of other factors, including the source of financing and the structure and culture of the organization sponsoring the innovation. These issues will be explored in our examination of the first group of research studies, namely those dealing with the valuation implications of innovation in general.

The specific questions I will address in reviewing this literature are as follows:

(1) Does innovation create shareholder value? What is the evidence on this?
(2) Why do firms do basic research that does not directly generate a product with revenue potential?
(3) How do companies set hurdle rates for innovative projects?
(4) How do innovative firms get financed?

Understanding the research insights on these questions will help us synthesize the existing body of knowledge on these issues and will also help us identify the open questions that still remain.

Financial innovation deals with the design and marketing of new types of financial securities and structures. Nobel laureate Merton Miller (1986) marveled at the period from the mid-1960s through the mid-1980s in asking: "Can any twenty-year period in recorded history have witnessed even a tenth as much (financial innovation)?" However, financial innovation has continued unabated since Miller made his observation. We have witnessed a dazzling array of new products — derivatives, exchange-traded funds (ETFs), variants of the tax-deductible equity, and securitization of all forms.

The questions that I will explore in reviewing this literature are as follows:

(1) How do we define financial innovation?
(2) Why have we observed so much financial innovation? What are the economic forces driving it?
(3) Who are the innovators, what are their incentives, and what is diffused in society?
(4) What are the social benefits of innovation?

The topic of financial innovation has been studied in some depth, so there are numerous excellent review articles that have been written on the subject. Examples include Allen and Gale (1994) and Tufano (2003). There are also numerous practitioner-oriented books on financial innovation, such as Crawford and Sen (1996) and Geanuracos and Millar (1991). Thus, I will not attempt to be exhaustive in my survey — the reader is referred to these other sources. Rather, I will selectively review the literature that helps me address the questions listed above.

The rest of this review is organized as follows. In Section 2, I discuss the research related to the four specific questions dealing with the valuation implications of innovation. In Section 3, I discuss the literature related to the four specific questions about financial innovation. Section 4 gathers all the key insights from the discussions in Sections 2 and 3. Section 5 concludes with a summary of unresolved issues and open questions.

2. Innovation and Shareholder Value: The Valuation Perspective

The purpose of this section is to discuss the literature that addresses the link between innovation and the financial valuation implications of this innovation for the sponsoring firms. As we will see, the literature on this topic has generated valuable insights, but it has also raised a plethora of unanswered questions that remain challenges — some quite formidable — for future research.

Does Innovation Create Shareholder Value?

This question is more difficult to answer than it might appear at first blush. It depends on how one interprets the question. If we interpret it as asking whether entrepreneurial activity that relies on innovation is value-maximizing (generating positive net present value) on average, then the answer appears to be no. Research has shown that on average, entrepreneurs earn lower expected returns than they should, given the amount of risk that they bear (see, for example, Bitler, Moskowitz and Vissing-Jørgensen (2005)). The psychological make-up of entrepreneurs is such that they are "excessively optimistic" and hence willing to accept risk-adjusted returns that others would not.

By contrast, if we take the perspective of society at large and ask the question of whether innovation is worthwhile for society, we get quite a different answer. For example, former President Bill Clinton states:

"Our passion for discovery, our determination to explore new scientific frontiers, and our can-do spirit of technological innovation has always driven this nation forward. Sustained investments in research can ensure that America remains at the forefront of scientific capability, thereby enhancing our ability to shape a more prosperous future for ourselves, our children, and future generations while building a better America for the twenty-first century."[1]

---

[1] Cited in Blazenko and Pavlov (forthcoming).

The research indicates that innovation *is* rewarded in the stock market, although not equally for all firms. In their book on the Competing Values Framework (CVF), Cameron, DeGraff, Quinn and Thakor (2006) examine the relationship between numerous forms of value creation, including innovation and stock market valuation. They find that there is a high statistical correlation between the variables of the Competing Values Framework and contemporaneous cross-sectional variations in the market-value-to-book-value ratios of (publicly-traded) companies. They find that innovation appears to be positively rewarded in the stock market, but the magnitude of the reward depends on the industry to which the firm belongs, and causality is hard to establish. Perhaps the easiest way to understand the managerial implications of their finding is to discuss the example of Hewlett-Packard given in the book. Cameron, DeGraff, Quinn and Thakor (2006) report that in the year 2000, Hewlett-Packard's performance in innovation was below the industry average. They calculate that a one-standard-deviation improvement in the innovation dimension for Hewlett-Packard may have resulted in an increase of $12.78 billion in market value.[2]

So, the bottom line is that innovation does seem to create shareholder value for firms, but the impact of innovation on value is industry-specific. Moreover, even though entrepreneurs on average may be inadequately rewarded in terms of return for the risk they take, their optimism leads to value-enhancing payoffs for society at large. However, Cameron, DeGraff, Quinn and Thakor (2006) also point out that the organizational forces that make innovative activities prosper within an organization also tend to pull the organization in a direction that is the opposite of efficiency. This raises interesting questions about potential tensions between efficiency and innovation.

Why Do Firms Do Basic Research?

The innovation we discussed above is what people think of as resulting from what is commonly referred to as "applied research," namely research

---

[2]Cameron, DeGraff, Quinn and Thakor (2006) examine a sample of over 3,000 publicly-traded firms. The one-standard-deviation measure is derived from the cross-sectional variation within this sample in the year 2000.

that is aimed primarily at producing goods and services that have revenue-generating potential for the firms that engage in it. It is easy to make a case for doing such applied research — it can enable the firm to generate product or service ideas that create a competitive advantage in the marketplace and lead to enhanced profit margins. An example would be the research and development (R&D) expenditures incurred by a pharmaceutical company. Such expenditures ultimately lead to patent-protected new drugs that are associated with relatively high profit margins.

But what about basic research? This research might, for example, be directed at testing new theories of quantum mechanics or developing new theories of financial market crises or unraveling the mysteries of the human genetic code. Such research is usually funded by government agencies like the National Science Foundation and the National Institute of Health. There is a reason for this. The ground-breaking papers by Arrow (1962) and Nelson (1959) make the important point that the private sector does not provide adequate incentives for investment in knowledge creation. There are numerous reasons for this, as explicated by Rosenberg (1990). First, basic research is characterized by substantial uncertainty and uninsurable risk. Second, there is a "free rider" problem in the production of knowledge via basic research — once knowledge is produced, it is relatively freely available to all, including those who contributed nothing to its production. Economists refer to this as an "appropriability" problem in the sense that firms financing the research lack adequate mechanisms for appropriating the benefits of the research to themselves. One could argue that it is the purpose of patents to provide this kind of protection. However, once knowledge has been generated via basic research, it is costlessly available for other firms to utilize, and any restrictions on its use are socially inefficient because it can deny productivity-enhancement opportunities to some firms without imposing any incremental cost on society.

Thus, a major conclusion of economic theory is that market incentives are insufficiently strong to generate the socially optimal amount of investment in basic research due to non-appropriability problems and high uncertainty.

This conclusion seems to be supported by the data. Most firms in the private sector do *not* conduct any basic research. Nonetheless, a few firms do engage in basic research. Rosenberg (1990) reports that in 1984, company-financed basic research amounted to $2.578 billion, of which 61% was concentrated in four sectors: chemicals, electrical equipment, aircraft and missiles, and machinery.

These data raise an obvious and interesting question: why do firms engage in basic research despite the high uncertainty and non-appropriability problems?

To this question, Rosenberg (1990) provides a thoughtful answer. I summarize it below as key factors that influence firms to conduct basic research:

(1) Large firms and those with substantial market power are more likely than other firms to invest in basic research. The reason is that the payoff from basic research is inherently long-term, so only firms that expect to be around in the long run will want to make the investment.

(2) Firms with more diverse ranges of products are more likely to engage in basic research. The reason is that the outcome of basic research is highly uncertain, so it is difficult to predict which product areas the outcome will be most useful for. The more diversified the range of products, the greater is the likelihood that the outcome of basic research will have a profitable commercial use.

(3) Firms often do not ask: should we do basic research? In this sense, a significant portion of the basic research that has been conducted by firms is *accidental*. In other words, "...basic research findings of major significance have emerged as the unplanned by-product of the attempt to solve some very specific industrial problem."[3] For example, if Louis Pasteur had been asked in 1870 what he was doing, he would have responded that he was trying to solve the fermentation and putre-faction problems in the French wine industry. Hardly esoteric basic research! In fact, Pasteur was addressing a very practical problem, and in doing so he invented the modern science of bacteriology. Similarly, the Frenchman Sadi Carnot created the modern science of thermodynamics while trying to improve the efficiency of steam

---

[3] See Rosenberg (1990).

engines. And Arno Penzias and Robert Wilson of Bell Labs were working on the very practical problem of signal loss in satellite communications when they observed the cosmic background radiation that was the first empirical verification of the "big bang" theory of the birth of the universe.[4]

(4) Investment in basic research is essentially like purchasing an option on the access to *future* knowledge. To see this, note that it takes a substantial capability to comprehend and interpret knowledge that is generated. Without in-house researchers and scientists, the firm will be unable to understand and appraise such knowledge. If its competitors are able to appraise it, they may be able to identify those pieces of knowledge that lead to commercially profitable innovations and thereby gain a potentially significant competitive advantage. So the firm may wish to maintain a group of in-house scientists and basic researchers, even though it is costly to do so. But you cannot keep such people idle. In order to maintain their skills, the firm has to be willing to allow them to engage in basic research. In other words, the best way to stay connected with the scientific network is to be an engaged participant in the process of basic research.

(5) Finally, the federal procurement process may also provide firms with incentives to do basic research. Take military procurement, for example. Firms that are in the defense contracting business will want to improve their odds of winning government contracts. One approach to improving one's chances is by conducting R&D that is relevant to the Department of Defense. The incentives to do so are strengthened by the federal government which sponsors design and technical competitions in which potential contractors participate, at least partially at their own expense.

Thus, we see that there are various factors that may encourage profit-maximizing firms to invest in basic research. These factors also provide prescriptive guidance to managers about the circumstances in which it may make sense for their firms to invest in basic research.

---

[4]Penzias and Wilson were awarded the Nobel Prize in Physics for their finding.

How Do Companies Set Hurdle Rates for Innovative Projects?

Investments in innovation, such as R&D, are difficult to evaluate using traditional capital budgeting approaches like net present value. To see this, consider the case of Hybritech, a biotech company that made medical diagnostic instruments and also was engaged in monoclonal-antibody research aimed at finding a cure for cancer, prior to its acquisition by Eli Lilly in the mid-1980s. How does a company like that evaluate the value of its R&D expenditure on finding a cure for cancer? Such expenditures have essentially binary payoff distributions — they either pay off a very large amount if the research is successful, or pay nothing if it is not successful.

Finance research has recognized that this makes R&D expenditures isomorphic to common stock options, so an investment in innovation can be viewed as the purchase of an option (see, for example, McDonald and Siegel (1986) and Dixit and Pindyck (1994)). This is an important insight because it points out that the "standard rules" that apply for normal or conventional investments need not apply for investments in innovation. In particular, for conventional investments, we know that an increase in payoff uncertainty leads to a reduction in the value of the project being financed, holding everything else constant. By contrast, because investments in innovation are like the purchase of "real options," an increase in payoff uncertainty *increases* the value of the (innovative) project.[5]

In line with this, Blazenko and Pavlov (forthcoming) have recently shown that, even though R&D has a development risk, making investments in R&D sequential and dependent on observed profitability can allow the firm to take advantage of the upside potential of R&D while limiting the downside risk.[6] Consequently, the hurdle rate for R&D-type projects may be *lower* than that for conventional investments.

---

[5]This follows from the well-known property of options, first identified by Black and Scholes (1972), that the value of the option is increasing in the volatility of the price of the underlying stock.

[6]There are numerous research papers on sequential investments. See Dixit and Pindyck (1994), Abel (1983), Pindyck (1988), Caballero (1991), and Aguerrevere (2003).

How Do Innovative Firms Get Financed?

There is a sizeable literature on how firms that arise to commercialize innovative ideas obtain the external financing they need to develop. This is the literature on venture capital financing, and it includes papers by Bottazzi, Da Rin and Hellmann (2008), Chan, Siegel and Thakor (1990), Hellmann and Puri (2000, 2002), Gompers (1995, 1996, 2006), Gompers and Lerner (1998), Kortum and Lerner (2000), and Tian and Wang (2009). These papers have examined various aspects of venture capital contracts and the link between innovation and venture capital financing from a theoretical as well as empirical perspective. As a result of this research, much has been learned about how venture capital firms operate and the various frictions in this market, as well as how contracts are designed to cope with these frictions. Some of these insights are summarized below:

- Optimal venture capital contracts contain provisions for transfer of control from the entrepreneur to the venture capitalist in such a way that the effective control given to the venture capitalist exceeds what might be suggested by the percentage of the firm owned by the venture capitalist.
- Venture capitalists tend to view their investments as comprising a portfolio of real options. Thus, they are willing to take substantial risks if there is sufficient *upside* potential.
- Venture capitalists help to "professionalize" the firms they finance. That is, the presence of a venture capitalist results in the entrepreneurial firm being staffed with more professionally-competent employees.
- Greater "failure tolerance" on the part of the venture capitalist is associated with greater innovation on the part of the firm that is financed.
- Bull markets tend to encourage venture capital financing because venture capitalists typically have an "exit strategy" when they finance entrepreneurs, and this involves taking the firm public through an initial public offering (IPO).

In addition to the venture capital literature, there is also a small but emerging literature on how compensation contracts should be written to motivate managers to engage in innovation. For example, Manso (2008) shows that the optimal contract to incentivize managers to invest in innovative activities involves a combination of tolerance for failures in the short run and reward for success in the long run.[7]

3. Financial Innovation

Let us now shift our attention from innovation in general to *financial* innovation, which deals with the emergence of new financial instruments. The economic motivation for these is typically linked to their contribution to improved risk management or enhanced liquidity for organizations and/ or individuals. So in this section, I discuss the literature that addresses the four questions related to financial innovation stated earlier.

How Do We Define Financial Innovation?

Tufano (2003) defines financial innovation as: "...the act of creating and popularizing new financial instruments, as well as new financial technologies, institutions and markets." Financial innovations can refer to both the creation of *new products* (e.g., new derivative contracts) and the creation of new processes for distributing securities, processing transactions, or pricing transactions.

There has been a veritable explosion of financial innovations in the past few decades that satisfy the definition above. For example, Finnerty (1988, 1992) and Finnerty and Emery (2001) list over 60 securities innovations. These innovations are organized by the type of instrument (debt, preferred stock, convertible securities and common stock) and by the function served (reallocating risk, increasing liquidity, reducing agency costs, reducing transaction costs, reducing taxes or circumventing regulatory constraints).

These are not the only ways to categorize financial innovations. There is, in fact, a large variety of ways in which people have attempted to create categories of financial innovations. Tufano (2003) mentions an investment bank that created a 64-page booklet that categorized the

---

[7] See also Hellmann and Thiele (2009).

characteristics of the innovative securities along five dimensions — coupons, life, redemption proceeds, issue price and warrants. The 1934 edition of the classic book by Dodd and Graham, *Security Analysis*, describes as many as 258 securities, including pay-in-kind bonds, step-up bonds, putable bonds, bonds with stock dividends, zero-coupon bonds, inflation-indexed bonds, various exotic convertible and exchangeable bonds, almost two dozen different types of warrants, voting bonds, non-voting shares, and so on.

Tufano (2003) mentions that his research revealed 1,836 unique "security codes" used from the early 1980s through early 2001 in the Thomson Financial Securities Data, a data vendor that tracks new security issuances. While some of the securities listed were just different names for virtually identical securities offered by other competitors, others represented refinements and improvements of previous products, and some were truly novel. This provides an indication of the sometimes frenetic pace of financial innovation activities.

In addition to these lists that contain corporate securities, there are also other financial innovations represented by exchange-traded derivatives, over-the-counter derivative contracts like credit derivatives, equity swaps and so on.

Why Have We Observed So Much Financial Innovation?

A number of perspectives have been offered on this question. Merton (1992) suggests that financial innovations are designed to help the financial system to better serve six functions: (1) moving funds across time and space; (2) pooling funds; (3) managing risk; (4) extracting information to support decision-making; (5) addressing moral hazard and asymmetric information problems; and (6) facilitating the sale and purchase of goods and services through a payment system.

To see how innovation can be described in these terms, consider asset securitization. It facilitates at least three of the above six functions: it pools mortgages, it modifies risk profiles through diversification, and it moves funds across time and space.

Tufano (2003) adopts a somewhat different perspective on why financial innovation occurs. He argues that innovations reflect responses to changes in the environment. Specifically, he provides the following reasons:

- **Innovations arise to reduce market incompleteness:** An incomplete market is defined as one in which not all states of nature are "spanned" by the available financial securities. Simply put, it means that no combination of existing securities can provide complete insurance against uncertainty. When markets are incomplete in this sense, the creation of a security that enables individuals to hedge previously unhedged risks is likely to be demanded by risk-averse individuals. A good example of a new security that helped to complete the market is Treasury STRIPS (separate trading of registered interest and principal securities) or zero-coupon bonds. Essentially, innovations like these that are designed to reduce market incompleteness seek to meet an unmet market demand or need.

- **Innovations arise to resolve agency and information problems:** Allen and Gale (1994) point out that some innovations help to resolve agency problems that arise from conflicts of interest between contracting parties, as well as asymmetric information problems that arise from one party to a contract knowing more than the other party and potentially benefitting from strategically exploiting this information advantage. For example, consider the options embedded in some innovative R&D financings.[8] In these structures, an R&D financing organization is set up with separate shareholders from the parent which retains all the decision rights with respect to the day-to-day management of this separate organization. In this setting, there is an inherent conflict of interest. The parent organization may wish to skimp on the provision of resources to the separate organization in such a way that the parent's value is enhanced at the expense of the separate organization. By attaching warrants exerciseable into the stock of the parent of the R&D financing vehicle, one partially attenuates this conflict of interest since the shareholders in the separate firm stand to gain from an increase in the value of the parent.

---

[8] See Lerner and Tufano (1993) for a case study of these innovations.

In addition to resolving agency problems, innovations also arise to diminish the frictions generated by asymmetric information. For example, in the 19th century, preferred stock was introduced that conditioned the voting rights of its holders on the firm's failure to comply with covenant terms.[9]

- **Innovations arise to reduce transaction, search or marketing costs:** Merton (1989) discusses how transaction costs can motivate specific innovations that help investors to lower these costs. An example of this is LYONS (liquid yield option notes); see McConnell and Schwartz (1992). Merrill Lynch observed that retail investors tended to put most of their money in low-risk securities and then purchase a series of call options. Merrill Lynch introduced LYONS to permit investors to replicate this payoff without having to incur the commission costs of rolling over their call option positions at least four times every year. Other examples of innovations that lower transaction costs are process innovations in payment systems — ATMs, ACH technologies, smart cards, etc. Tufano (2003) notes that these innovations could lower transaction costs by a factor of over 100.

  Other examples are business model innovations that also seek to lower transaction costs — Instinet, OpenIPO, EnronOnline, eBay and various business-to-business (B2B) exchanges.

- **Innovations arise in response to taxes and regulation:** Merton Miller (1986) made his famous remark on this over 20 years ago when he observed, "The major impulses to successful innovations over the past twenty years have come, I am saddened to say, from regulation and taxes." Examples of such tax-induced innovations are plenty: zero-coupon bonds, trust-preferred structures, Eurodollar Eurobonds and so on.

  On the connection between regulation and innovation, firms often come up with innovations to circumvent "regulatory taxes." Kane (1986) describes the "regulatory dialectic" as a major source of innovation. He provides examples from banking. Banks view capital

---

[9] See Dewing (1934).

requirements as costly,[10] and thus innovations arise to help banks reduce the amount of capital they must hold. Examples include capital notes and perpetual, non-cumulative preferred stock that qualify as regulatory capital, as well as 364-day loan commitments that allow banks to avoid having to hold capital that would be needed to support loan commitments with maturities of one year or greater.

- **Increasing globalization and risk motivate innovation:** Globalization exposes firms to currency and geopolitical risk. Various innovations have emerged to help companies manage these risks. For example, the Inter-American Development Bank has created an instrument that incorporates a currency convertibility and transferability guarantee. Other innovations have arisen to meet the specific needs of investors in a particular country. For example, there are structures designed to appeal to investors in a Japanese insurance company — these structures provide a form of cross-national regulatory arbitrage (see Tufano (2003)).

  Increasing volatility has also been a driver of innovation. Foreign exchange futures, swaps and options, swaptions, interest rate futures, and commodity swaps are all examples of this. In an earlier time period, when there was high inflation uncertainty, products to hedge against this uncertainty arose. For example, "stabilized" (inflation-indexed) bonds were introduced after World War I in 1925; these bonds linked interest and principal payments to the wholesale price index.[11]

- **Technological shocks stimulate innovation:** Whenever information technology advances, it permits the introduction of new financial products that permit increasingly finer partitions of risks to be hedged. For example, advances in information technology have played a role in the design of securitization structures that involve a large number

---

[10]The economics underlying bankers' aversion to capital remain somewhat elusive, however, even though this may seem obvious to the layperson. Mehran and Thakor (2011) show that bank value is actually *increasing* in capital, and banks that keep *higher* levels of capital seem to do *better* for their shareholders. This makes it somewhat perplexing why one so often hears of the aversion bankers display toward keeping higher capital.

[11] See Masson and Stratton (1938).

of tranches, with each tranche catering to the demands of a potentially different investor clientele. Other examples include new methods of securities underwriting (e.g., OpenIPO), new methods of assembling portfolios of stocks (FOLIOfn), new markets for securities and new ways of executing securities transactions.

While I have discussed various factors as being potential drivers of financial innovation, in practice many of these factors work in concert to spawn innovations. For example, market funds, index funds, ETFs (exchange-traded funds), HOLDRs (holding company depository receipts), and personal funds are motivated by possibly all of the factors discussed above.

Who are the Innovators and What are Their Incentives?

Innovation is often introduced by financial institutions who perceive certain benefits from innovation. The theoretical argument for innovation has been developed in numerous academic research papers. Ross (1989) proposes that investment banks come up with innovations to reduce marketing or search costs. Boot and Thakor (1997) show that a "functionally separated" financial system — one in which investment and commercial banks are separated by regulatory fiat as during the Glass–Steagall era in the US — will have investment banks that are more innovative than what one would encounter in a universal banking system. The idea is that innovation is retarded in a universal banking system because any market-based innovation by an investment bank within a universal banking system potentially cannibalizes a product offered by the commercial bank within the universal bank. Since such cannibalization concerns do not exist in a functionally-separated system, there is greater innovation in such a system. More recently, Thakor (2012) has developed a model in which financial institutions come up with "unfamiliar" innovations — those that involve potential disagreement among different institutions about their market potential — as a way to limit the number of imitators and hence protect their profit margins due to the reduced competition.

There is also academic research which indicates that the firms that are most likely to innovate are those that are the most constrained or adversely affected by existing market conditions. In other words, innovation is more likely to come from smaller firms. There is anecdotal evidence to support this. The Vanguard Group and Drexel Burnham Lambert, both new financial service firms at the time, grew via innovative products like junk bonds and index funds. However, the large-sample empirical evidence appears to go in the *opposite* direction. Tufano (1989) shows that the more financially-secure investment banks have been the leading innovators, and Matthews (1994) explains why. One possible reason is that larger, better established financial service firms may have greater credibility and reach in convincing potential customers to adopt their innovation, so successful introductions of innovations may be easier for such financial-service firms.

How do innovations spread through the system? The literature on industrial organizations has studied extensively the issue of diffusion of innovations (e.g., Molyneux and Shamroukh (1999)). This literature has focused mainly on the question of which organizations adopt innovations and how rapidly. Although there is a rich variety of findings in this literature, an important conclusion appears to be that larger firms have innovated more rapidly, and that their innovations have also been diffused more rapidly through the financial system. An example is the more rapid adoption of credit scoring models for credit analysis by larger banks.

What are the Social Benefits of Innovation?

Innovation clearly has the potential to enhance value creation through a variety of means. Tufano (2003) discusses a book by Geanuracos and Millar (1991), *The Power of Financial Innovation*, which studies 75 firms around the world. This book concludes that the world's best-run companies are making the most effective use of the latest innovations.

Financial innovations have the potential to benefit society in the following two ways. First, they lower the cost of capital for firms, so firms are able to invest in more projects, achieve higher growth and contribute to an increase in global gross domestic product (GDP) and wealth. Second, they permit more risks to be borne in the financial markets, thereby providing access to capital for a wider array of needs. Mortgages securitization is an example of both benefits working in concert. Securitization enabled the mortgage market to become liquid, thereby lowering liquidity risk for originating banks, giving these banks access to the capital market for funding, and reducing the cost of borrowing for home buyers (see Hendershott and Shilling (1989) and Benjamin and Sirmans (1990)).[12]

A big issue in financial innovation is that it can typically *not* be patented like other innovations. Financial innovations have generally been viewed as "business processes," which are hard to patent. Tufano (2003) points out, however, that in 1998 the Federal Circuit Court of Appeals ruled in the State Street Bank v. Signature Financial 47 USPQ2d (BNA) 1596 (Fed. Cir. 1998) that Signature's patent of its "Hub-and-Spokes" system for asset management was protected intellectual property. It is not clear yet how broadly this decision will be interpreted, but Lerner (2002) has documented that financial patenting activity is on the rise. The implications of this for financial innovation and for society at large remain unclear at this stage.

4. Summary of Key Insights

It is difficult to present a really neat summary of such a big topic, given the voluminous amount of research that has been done on it. However, here is a sampling of the key insights[13]:

- Innovation has the potential to create shareholder value, but the magnitude of the potential impact depends on the industry context.
- The organizational forces that encourage innovation may impede efficiency and vice versa.
- Firms often engage in basic research, either accidentally while attempting to solve applied problems, or because it gives them in-house capabilities to interpret and adopt new ideas in technically complex fields.

---

[12] Whether financial innovation improves social welfare is not a settled issue in research. Allen and Gale (1994) and Elul (1995) provide examples of situations in which innovations may reduce welfare.

[13] Since these are insights based primarily on academic research, there is considerable scope for translating these into practical and actionable decision rules for managers.

- Larger and financially sounder firms are more likely to engage in basic research, and larger and financially-sounder financial service firms are more likely to introduce financial innovations.
- Firms with more diverse ranges of products are more likely to engage in basic research.
- For capital budgeting purposes, innovative projects should be viewed as "real options." This approach can lead to hurdle rates for innovative projects being *lower* than those for conventional projects.
- Innovative firms are financed by venture capitalists who tend to view their investments as comprising a portfolio of real options. This induces them to invest in relatively risky firms.
- Venture capitalists help to professionalize the firms they finance.
- Greater failure tolerance on the part of the venture capitalist is associated with greater innovation on the part of the firm that is financed.
- Bull stock markets tend to encourage venture capital financing.
- There has been an explosion in financial innovations in the past 40 years, and the pace is not slowing down. There is a plethora of motivating economic factors, including globalization, regulation and technological advances.
- While financial innovation is generally believed to benefit society by lowering costs of capital and making financing available for riskier ventures, the issue of the social benefits of financial innovation is still unsettled.

5. Conclusion

This survey paper has attempted to summarize a large body of work in academic research dealing with the financial aspects of innovation and with financial innovation. The survey has yielded a rich harvest of insights, but many open questions remain for future research.

First, to the extent that both efficiency and innovation contribute to shareholder value, and there is a tension between the two, what are the most effective organizational responses for resolving the tension? This continues to be a major challenge for practicing managers. The Competing Values Framework (CVF) developed by Cameron, DeGraff, Quinn and

Thakor (2006) offers various tools to resolve these tensions in practice. But more work is needed on this.

Second, what are the pros and cons of making a broad class of financial innovations patentable? This is a complex issue that does not have straightforward answers. Given the absence of patenting, the answer seems to be that innovation can reduce stability, but this is a very preliminary finding that needs to be explored further from a variety of perspectives.

Third, what is the relationship between financial innovation and financial stability? While on the one hand, patenting will slow down the spread of practice-based knowledge across firms, the recent research by Thakor (2012) suggests that it may also improve financial stability.

Finally, how should managers decide on the optimal allocation of resources across mundane and innovative organizational activities, and how should organizational structure adapt?

Future research will hopefully shed light on these issues.

References

Abel, Andrew B., "Optimal Investment Under Uncertainty", *American Economic Review* 73-1, 1983, pp. 228–233.

Aguerrevere, Felipe, "Equilibrium Investment Strategies and Output Price Behavior: A Real-Options Approach", *Review of Financial Studies* 16-4, 2003, pp. 1239–1272.

Allen, Franklin, and Douglas Gale, *Financial Innovation and Risk Sharing*, MIT Press: Cambridge, MA, 1994.

Arrow, Kenneth, "Economic Welfare and the Allocation of Resources for Invention", in *The Rate and Direction of Inventive Activity*, edited by R.R. Nelson, Princeton University Press: Princeton, NJ, 1962, pp. 609–625.

Benjamin, John D., and C.F. Sirmans, "Pricing Fixed Rate Mortgages: Some Empirical Evidence", *Journal of Financial Services Research* 4-3, 1990, pp. 191–202.

Bitler, Marianne P., Tobias J. Moskowitz and Annette Vissing-Jørgensen, "Testing Agency Theory with Entrepreneur Effort and Wealth", *Journal of Finance* 60-2, 2005, pp. 539–576.

Black, Fischer, and Myron S. Scholes, "The Valuation of Option Contracts and a Test of Market Efficiency", *Journal of Finance* 27-2, 1972, pp. 399–418.

Blazenko, George W., and Andrey D. Pavlov, "Value Maximizing Hurdle Rates for R&D Investment", *Economics of Innovation and New Technology*, forthcoming.

Boot, Arnoud W.A., and Anjan V. Thakor, "Banking Scope and Financial Innovation", *Review of Financial Studies* 10-4, 1997, pp. 1099–1131.

Bottazzi, Laura, Marco Da Rin and Thomas Hellmann, "Who are the Active Investors? Evidence from Venture Capital", *Journal of Financial Economics* 89-3, 2008, pp. 488–812.

Caballero, Ricardo, "On the Sign of the Investment-Uncertainty Relationship", *American Economic Review* 81-1, 1991, pp. 279–288.

Cameron, Kim S., Jeff DeGraff, Robert E. Quinn and Anjan V. Thakor, *Competing Values Leadership: Creating Value in Organizations*, Edward Elgar: Northampton, MA, 2006.

Chan, Yuk-Shee, Daniel Siegel and Anjan V. Thakor, "Learning, Corporate Control and Performance Requirements in Venture Capital Contracts", *International Economic Review* 31-2, 1990, pp. 365–381.

Crawford, George, and Bidyut Sen, *Derivatives for Decision Makers: Strategic Management Issues*, John Wiley & Sons: New York, 1996.

Dewing, A.S., *Study of Corporate Securities*, Ronald Press: New York, 1934.

Dixit, Avinash K., and Robert S. Pindyck, *Investment Under Uncertainty*, Princeton University Press: Princeton, NJ, 1994.

Dodd, David, and Benjamin Graham, *Security Analysis*, McGraw-Hill, 1934.

Elul, Ronel, "Welfare Effects of Financial Innovation in Incomplete Market Economies with Several Consumption Goods", *Journal of Economic Theory* 65, 1995, pp. 43–78.

Finnerty, John D., "An Overview of Corporate Securities Innovation", *Journal of Applied Corporate Finance* 4-4, 1992, pp. 23–39.

Finnerty, John D., "Financial Engineering in Corporate Finance: An Overview", *Financial Management* 17, 1988, pp. 14–33.

Finnerty, John D., and Douglas R. Emery, *Debt Management: A Practitioner's Guide*, Harvard University Press: Cambridge, MA, 2001.

Geanuracos, John, and Bill Millar, *The Power of Financial Innovation: Successful Corporate Solutions to Managing Interest Rate, Foreign Exchange Rate and*

Commodity Exposures on a Worldwide Basis, Harper Business Press: New York, 1991.

Gompers, Paul A., "Venture Capital and Private Equity", in *Handbook of Corporate Finance: Empirical Corporate Finance*, edited by Espen Eckbo, Elsevier/North-Holland: New York, 2006.

Gompers, Paul A., "Grandstanding in the Venture Capital Industry", *Journal of Financial Economics* 42-1, 1996, pp. 133–156.

Gompers, Paul A., "Optimal Investment, Monitoring and the Staging of Venture Capital", *Journal of Finance* 50-5, 1995, pp. 1461–1489.

Gompers, Paul, and Josh Lerner, "Venture Capital Distributions: Short-run and Long-run Reactions", *Journal of Finance* 53-6, 1998, pp. 2161–2183.

Hellmann, Thomas, and Manju Puri, "Venture Capital and Professionalization of Start-up Firms: Empirical Evidence", *Journal of Finance* 15-1, 2002, pp. 169–197.

Hellmann, Thomas, and Manju Puri, "The Interaction between Product Market and Financing Strategy: The Role of Venture Capital", *Review of Financial Studies* 13-4, 2000, pp. 959–984.

Hellmann, Thomas, and Veikko Thiele, "Incentives and Innovation: A Multi-tasking Approach", University of British Columbia working paper, 2009.

Hendershott, Patric H., and James D. Shilling, "The Impact of Agencies on Conventional Fixed-Rate Mortgage Yields", *Journal of Real Estate Finance and Economics* 2-2, 1989, pp. 101–115.

Kane, Edward J., "Technology and the Regulation of Financial Markets", in *Technology and the Regulation of Financial Markets, Securities, Futures and Banking*, edited by Anthony Saunders and Lawrence J. White, Lexington Books: Lexington, MA, 1986, pp. 187–193.

Kortum, Samuel, and John Lerner, "Assessing the Contribution of Venture Capital to Innovation", *Rand Journal of Economics* 31-4, 2000, pp. 674–692.

Lerner, Josh, "Where Does State Street Lead? A First Look at Finance Patents, 1971–2000", *Journal of Finance* 57-2, 2002, pp. 901–903.

Lerner, Josh, and Peter Tufano, "ALZA and Bio-Electrical Systems (A) Technological and Financial Innovation", HBS Case No. 293124, 1993, Harvard Business Publishing, http://harvardbusiness.org/product/alza-and-bio-electro-systems-a-technological-and-f/an/293124-PDF-ENG?N=4294936347&Ntt=financial+strategy.

Manso, Gustavo, "Motivating Innovation", MIT Sloan School of Management working paper, 2008.

Masson, Robert L., and Samuel S. Stratton, *Financial Instruments and Institutions: A Case Book*, McGraw-Hill: New York, 1938.

Matthews, John O., *Struggle and Survival on Wall Street*, Oxford University Press: New York, 1994.

McConnell, John J., and Eduardo S. Schwartz, "The Origin of LYONs: A Case Study in Financial Innovation", *Journal of Applied Corporate Finance* 4-4, 1992, pp. 40–47.

McDonald, Robert, and Daniel Siegel, "The Value of Waiting to Invest", *Quarterly Journal of Economics* 101-4, 1986, pp. 707–728.

Mehran, Hamid, and Anjan V. Thakor, "Bank Capital and Value in the Cross Section", *Review of Financial Studies* 24-4, 2011, pp. 1021–1255.

Merton, Robert C., "On the Application of the Continuous-Time Theory of Finance to Financial Intermediation and Insurance", *The Geneva Papers on Risk and Insurance* 14-3, 1989, pp. 225–261.

Miller, Merton H., "Financial Innovation: The Last Twenty Years and the Next", *Journal of Financial and Quantitative Analysis* 21-4, 1986, pp. 459–471.

Molyneux, Philip, and Nidal Shamroukh, *Financial Innovation*, John Wiley & Sons: West Sussex, England, 1999.

Nelson, Richard, "The Simple Economics of Basic Scientific Research", *Journal of Political Economy* 67-3, 1959, pp. 297–306.

Pindyck, Robert, "Irreversible Investment, Capacity Choice and the Value of the Firm", *American Economic Review* 78-5, 1988, pp. 969–985.

Rosenberg, Nathan, "Why Do Firms Do Basic Research (with Their Own Money)?", *Research Policy* 19-2, 1990, pp. 165–174.

Ross, Stephen A., "Institutional Markets, Financial Marketing and Financial Innovation", *Journal of Finance* 44-3, 1989, pp. 541–556.

State Street Bank v. Signature Financial Group, U.S. Court of Appeals for the Federal Circuit, 47 USPQ2d (BNA) 1596 (Fed. Cir. 1998), http://www.ll. georgetown.edu/federal/judicial/fed/caseBrowse.cfm?caseYear=1998#S.

Thakor, Anjan V., "Incentives to Innovate and Financial Crises", *Journal of Financial Economics* 103-1, 2012, pp. 130–148.

Tian, Xuan, and Tracy Y. Wang, "Tolerance for Failure and Corporate Innovation", Indiana University working paper, 2009.

Tufano, Peter, "Financial Innovation: The Last 200 Years and the Next", in *The Handbook of Economics of Finance*, edited by George M. Constantinides, Milton Harris and René M. Stulz, Elsevier/North-Holland: Amsterdam, 2003, pp. 307–335.

Tufano, Peter, "Financial Innovation and First-Mover Advantages", *Journal of Financial Economics* 25-2, 1989, pp. 213–240.

Part B:

Innovation Perspectives for Managers

Chapter 5

Creating a Climate for Business Innovation: Guidelines for Leaders

Lee J. Konczak

Academic Director, Executive MBA Program and Senior Lecturer,
Organizational Behavior & Leadership Development,
Olin Business School, Washington University in St. Louis

Signe Spencer

Senior Consultant, Hay Group

Recent data suggest that innovation is a high priority amongst senior executives. How can leaders create an environment to foster business innovation? This chapter introduces a framework that leaders can apply to facilitate innovation in their organizations. The framework stresses the importance of organizational climate and how it can support — or undermine — innovation.

1. Introduction

Examine the list of companies in Table 1. Although they represent a wide range of industries, these companies share one characteristic that gives them a competitive advantage in the marketplace. What important characteristic do they share?

All of the companies listed ranked in the top 10 of *Fortune*'s annual roster of the World's Most Admired Companies (The World's Most Admired Companies, 2012). And they share in common an important characteristic that is becoming increasingly important in today's turbulent business environment: the ability to innovate. More specifically, these 10 companies are able to introduce new products and services, expand into new markets, and make incremental improvements to existing products, services and processes in a way that differentiates them from their competitors and provides an

Table 1. World's most admired companies

Apple	FedEx
Google	Berkshire Hathaway
Amazon	Starbucks
Coca-Cola	Procter & Gamble
IBM	Southwest Airlines

important edge in good times and bad times alike. A few examples of how these companies deliver innovation to the marketplace are described below.

Apple

As a new product, the iPod transformed the music industry, and its appeal transcended gender, age, and ethnicity in its ability to enable users to listen to the music of their choice wherever they may be and whenever the urge moves them. In 2007, half of Apple's revenues were generated by music and the iPod. The company followed this performance in 2008 with the iPhone with tremendous success. The iPad, introduced in early 2010, represented the next wave of product innovation, followed by the introduction of the iPad Mini in 2012.

FedEx

FedEx introduced the Smart Package as a new service to safeguard the shipment of delicate goods such as human organs. The Smart Package is wired so that both the shipper and the recipient can easily track its location and its condition (e.g., temperature and humidity) and to receive an alert in the event of damage. FedEx remains among the leaders in the package delivery industry.

Southwest Airlines

Southwest Airlines changed its boarding procedures several years ago to allow reserved seating while remaining ticketless. Additionally, the airline added a deluxe program to retain high-revenue business passengers. Southwest has continued to expand its routes in the US despite challenging economic times.

2. Innovation for Growth

The examples cited above illustrate the importance of innovation for creating competitive advantage and facilitating a company's growth. Recent studies by the Boston Consulting Group (Andrew, Haanaes, Michael, Sirkin and Taylor, 2007, 2008, 2009; Andrew, Manget, Michael, Taylor and Zablit, 2010) provide further insight concerning the extent to which companies around the globe are focusing their resources on innovation — and some of the challenges they are experiencing in their efforts.

Based on the 2010 global survey of over 1,500 senior executives representing virtually all major industries, key results suggested that:

- Innovation is a strategic priority for a majority of companies, with 72% of respondents ranking it among their top three priorities;
- Sixty-one percent of respondents said their companies planned to increase spending on innovation (up from 58% in 2009);
- Satisfaction with the results of innovation is mixed. While 59% of C-level executives were satisfied with the return on innovation investments, slightly more than half of directors and managers and only 36% of other employees expressed satisfaction.

Companies are spending more on innovation, but, at the same time, many are not satisfied with the results they are achieving from that expenditure. What factors seemed to account for dissatisfaction with innovation efforts? Table 2 shows an abbreviated listing of the innovation capabilities with which respondents felt *least* satisfied (Andrew *et al.*, 2009). As you

Table 2. Innovation capabilities with which respondents felt least satisfied

Innovation Capability	Least Satisfied*
Moving quickly from idea generation to execution	45
Enforcing timelines and milestones	41
Partnering with others for new ideas	38
Fostering a culture of innovation	38
Ensuring executive-level support	31

*Percentage of respondents who said "Below Average" or "Poor".

review the table, keep this question in mind: What role do leaders play when it comes to these types of capabilities?

These data suggest that a significant proportion of the employees in the respondent companies may be experiencing the following reactions in their work environment:

- a lack of understanding about how quickly they need to move projects forward;
- a weak sense of accountability for results;
- a lack of participation and involvement in innovation efforts;
- a company atmosphere that may not respond openly to new ideas;
- a lack of adequate support for team innovation efforts.

Increasing budgets aimed at innovation will not directly influence or change employee experiences like those listed above. The focus of this chapter is to address the following key questions: (1) What role do *leaders* play in shaping such employee reactions and experiences? And (2) How might these survey responses look if leaders behaved differently?

The negative experiences described above are all indicators of what organizational psychologists refer to as *organizational climate*. From an employee's perspective, organizational climate has to do with the following questions: What is it like to work here? How does my experience while at work influence my willingness to work hard and put forth extra effort to ensure my team's success?

Organizational climate, as it is discussed in this chapter, refers to employees' perceptions of how it feels to work in a particular setting. It is largely determined by the behaviors of the local leader, and may vary dramatically from one work-unit to another within the same organization. In this way it is different from organizational culture which is a much broader, more enduring characteristic of an organization. An individual manager or leader may not be able to have a strong impact on the overall culture but can change the climate for his/her work-unit, for better or for worse.

Organizational climate describes six dimensions focusing on "the way we do things here" *that directly affect employees' ability to perform*. These six dimensions are described in Table 3. Research over the past 40 years has shown that organizational climate is related to various

Table 3. Organizational climate: The six ways that employees experience their organization that support their ability to produce excellent results

Climate Dimension	Employees' Perceptions
Clarity	It is clear what is expected and how that relates to the larger goals and objectives of the organization. The purpose and meaning of the work is clear.
Flexibility	New ideas are welcome and are easily accepted; there are few or no unnecessary rules, policies and procedures.
Responsibility	Employees have autonomy and authority delegated to them. They can do their work without excess interference. They can take reasonable business risks.
Team Commitment	People like and trust their co-workers because everyone is working together toward a common objective. People give extra effort to help each other when needed. They are proud to belong to this organization.
Standards	Management emphasizes improving performance. Management sets challenging but attainable goals for the organization and for employees.
Rewards	Excellent work is recognized and rewarded. Recognition and reward is directly related to the level of performance, so the best performance is the most strongly rewarded.

business outcomes — employee motivation and discretionary effort, team commitment as well as quality, productivity, financial results — and innovation (Hay Group, 2008).

What are the antecedents of organizational climate? Research indicates that one of the key drivers of organizational climate is leadership — *what* leaders do and *how* they do it (Goleman, 2000). More specifically, a leader's behavior with respect to establishing direction, setting goals, monitoring performance, giving feedback, and interacting with teams has a direct influence on organizational climate, which in turn has a direct impact on results. How can you, as a leader, modify the organizational climate your employees experience to enhance the innovation efforts of your team? These are the questions we will address in the subsequent sections of this chapter; but prior to doing that, let us take a few moments to discuss what we mean by innovation.

3. Innovation Defined

According to Webster, innovation is: a new idea, method or device; a novelty. This definition is a bit broad when it comes to application, so we take it a bit further and define innovation as: new ideas that are useful to other people. More specifically, innovation has to involve new ideas that are *executable* — they can be taken to market — and that are *perceived to be of value by others* (Gardner, 1993). In other words, customers have to be willing to "buy" them.

What Type of Innovation is Needed?

Before we turn our attention to a more detailed discussion of organizational climate and leadership, there is one final question that we need to ask. That is: What type of innovation is needed? From our previous discussion of examples of innovation at companies like Apple and Southwest Airlines at the beginning of this chapter, we observed that innovation can take an array of forms. Having an understanding of the type of innovation you are hoping to achieve will make a difference with respect to the organizational climate that will be most effective. As a tool to answer this question, the Continuum of Innovation (see Figure 1) will help you to

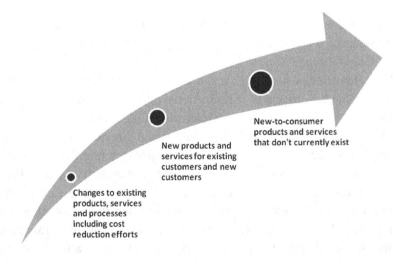

New-to-consumer
products and services
that don't currently exist

New products and
services for existing
customers and new
customers

Changes to existing
products, services
and processes
including cost
reduction efforts

Figure 1.   Continuum of innovation

clarify the innovation you are seeking and the leadership actions you need to take to achieve the outcomes you desire. The kind of innovation needed — and the amount of associated change the organization is willing to accept — is a strategic decision you should discuss with your own boss and peers. Incremental innovation, depicted on the left side of Figure 1, fits well into the way the organization currently works and will generally require less change to implement (i.e., it is "paradigm-consistent"). In contrast, "new-to-consumer" innovations may challenge existing paradigms (paradigm-breaking) and require more significant changes in the organization. As a leader, you need to be reasonably clear, yourself, about the amount and kinds of innovative changes you are prepared to welcome and encourage. This clarity will enable you to create a climate that will foster the kinds of innovations needed (Kirton, 1994).

4. Understanding the Innovation–Organizational Climate Linkage

Business innovation is most often a team effort — many people feel they "own" the idea. As an example, in the early 1990s, Hay Group worked with a company in which there had recently been a big and successful innovation in the way the company understood its role and its business model. The change was comparable to moving from "we are a buggy-whip company" to "we are a fine leather-goods company". As we interviewed executives, we found six who each claimed this idea as their own. We were pretty sure we knew who had actually come up with the idea (the person who could provide details about the context and how they came up with this idea). The important insight for innovation is that the other five executives were not deliberately misleading us — they really did feel personal ownership for the idea. And, the person who had the original insight could not have made it happen on his own. It was crucial to the success of this innovation that each leader truly felt "it was my idea" because then they were all committed to making it happen. Each of them had important insights and contributions to the realization of the idea, even if not in the original conception.

Just like how "it takes a village to raise a child", it really does take a whole team to bring an original idea to market. Thinking about the team and team/organizational climate is essential; business innovation is rarely a product of the "lonely eccentric genius". A recent study of innovative applied scientists — whom everyone described as loners — revealed that while they did often work alone, all the best and most important innovations were the result of close collaboration, not of solitary flashes of brilliance (Hay Group, 2009). Because of the importance of team or group efforts in business innovation, the leader's role is more to create the conditions for the team to be innovative than it is to be single-handedly innovative.

In the following sections of this chapter, we will address how the leader can create a climate in which the team can be innovative. We will expand on the framework presented earlier in the chapter that targets the organizational climate dimensions that the leader must attend to in order to help the team to be generally productive and innovative in their work.

Our framework entails several implicit assumptions. Essentially, innovation is a form of "discretionary effort" — leaders can push, prod or pay people to produce work, but they cannot force them to come up with useful new ideas. And, the harder one tries to "push" innovation, the less insightful and the less useful the results will be. The leader has to create a sense of "psychological safety" in which employees feel free to think of new ideas, and feel safe in sharing them (Edmondson, 1999). We can get a sense of how the leadership accomplishes these tasks by understanding in more detail the dimensions of the organizational climate that leaders create.

5. Dimensions of Organizational Climate

The **Clarity** dimension of organizational climate measures the sense employees have that they know what is expected of them and how those expectations relate to the larger goals and objectives of the organization. They feel they understand the overall organizational vision and the plans to achieve it, and they understand the structure, roles and efficient functioning of the organization. Clarity is the climate dimension with the strongest direct impact on productivity.

Often, increasing people's sense of clarity is simply a matter of taking the time and effort to explain, not only "what" to do, but also "why". Although explaining the context takes a bit of time at the moment, it saves time in the long run, as people are more likely to make the appropriate judgments and decisions as they implement the "what to do".

To foster innovation, you need to create *Clarity specifically about innovation. As a leader, you must create a mindset for innovation.* Your desire for innovation and the ways it could enhance your organization's mission needs to be an important content in your communications. You need to communicate how innovation fits into the larger purpose of your company and how it will be managed organizationally, not just Clarity about the work as it is now. To get the most innovative results, the kind of clarity you provide needs to be matched to the kind of innovation you need. A sense of the overall importance of one's work and the potential innovations can be very inspiring, but you also need to point people in the right direction.

To support innovation, the leader must address the following questions frequently and with consistency, even when they are not explicitly asked:

- Where is this organization heading? How does my team fit in with the intended direction?
- What kind of innovation does the organization want from our unit? What difference will it make to us? To the organization? To the larger world?
- What are the boundaries of our innovation? (Anything goes? Anything within the same industry? Within the same product? Paradigm-consistent or not?)
- What kinds of resources are available for innovations: How much time? Money? Cooperation from other units?
- Am I doing the right things, working on the right new ideas, to support our organization? (If not, what should I be doing differently?)
- How does my job fit into the innovation picture?

In some situations, creating clarity is a bigger and more crucial task. These questions cannot be answered in a healthy and sustainable way without being *aligned with the larger organization, and this alignment is the manager's responsibility*, at every level of the organization. As a manager, part of your role in creating clarity is to understand the direction of the larger organization, and to build the connections and alignments with other functions or units so that your group's new ideas will be well-focused on the needs of the organization and the customers, and so that the benefits of the innovations can be realized. This task can go beyond clear communication to include building a clear and practical structure for your part of the organization.

Recently, we worked with an organization where a talented R&D unit was building interesting new products. Unfortunately, this unit was not aligned with the sales department. The result was that the R&D unit was deprived of insight into which innovations would be most highly valued by customers, and the sales unit did not really try to sell the new products. The new leader immediately set about repairing the breach between his unit and his peer who was responsible for sales. He initiated meetings and enhanced practical communication between his group and the salespeople, creating more alignment and clarity for both groups. This leader carried the alignment question even further when he realized that, within his department, the roles were not well-organized to produce the kind of innovations that the customers, the sales group and the larger organization needed. Instead of keeping the work organized by the technology platforms, he reorganized the group by type of customer need, cutting across the technology platforms. This change was more efficient, focused the developers more strongly on customer needs, and sped up innovation by cross-fertilization between groups addressing similar problems. This kind of internal alignment to the innovation that is needed (in this case, moderately new customer-facing innovation) is an important part of creating Clarity.

If you are interested in "paradigm-consistent" innovation, you will need to make the areas of innovation you are interested in fairly clear. *The more "out there" the innovation, the wider the aperture you need to set.* To inspire more paradigm-breaking innovation, you might muse on areas of unmet needs for your customers or in the market.

Many of the best Indian CEOs are particularly adept at inspiring "paradigm-breaking" innovations (Spencer, Rajah, Narayan, Mohan and Lahiri, 2007). As an example, one leader of an Indian bank kept saying things like "the villagers could really benefit from our banking services to help them get out of desperate poverty — but their individual deposits would be too small to pay for the processing and we can't put a branch in every village....What could we do instead?" Another CEO thought out loud about the farmers who supplied his company: "We're not getting the quality of beans we need and the supply is uneven. Meanwhile the farmers are spending way too much time going to market and then waiting for the middleman and often not getting the best price because there was too much available that day." In both cases, the ultimate outcome was a new business model (a paradigm-breaking innovation) that met the needs of the market and of the company. The bank set up a version of "micro-financing" in which a group of women in each village learned about saving and making loans, and had a single savings-and-loan account for their group, where they deposited all their savings and from which they made each other loans under the guidance of the bank. The agricultural company set up an Internet kiosk in each village (in the home of a farmer who took on certain leadership responsibilities) that enabled the farmers to learn how to improve the quality of their beans, and when to take them to market for the best price and therefore the most even flow to the company.

Clarity Questions to ask as a leader:

- Does my team know what our mission and direction is and *why it is important*? Do they agree?
- Do I take the time to explain the reason behind decisions, directions or requests? Or do I tend to short-cut the explanations, with a "just do it because I said so" attitude?
- Do I set aside enough time for my team to consider and work on innovative ideas?
- Does my team know how much innovation I would welcome? What kinds of innovations?
- Does my team have an understanding of how innovations could improve the company and their own work lives?

Flexibility reflects people's feelings about the constraints imposed by the environment. It includes two aspects: (1) the degree to which the workplace is free of unnecessary rules, procedures, and policies; and (2) the feeling that new ideas are welcome and are easily accepted. Flexibility and Clarity work hand-in-hand to define the boundaries within which to innovate.

The connection between a sense of Flexibility and a willingness to share new ideas is so obvious that the second aspect of Flexibility is often called "innovation", and obviously Flexibility is needed to encourage employees to come up with novel ideas. But there is more to creating a sense of Flexibility than just saying "new ideas are welcome". The leader must actually welcome those ideas, and must respond in a constructive manner to the inevitable setbacks, disappointments and blind alleys that accompany any truly innovative endeavor. The leader must set an example of openness to learning and to new ideas. Nothing is more de-motivating than a leader who says new ideas are welcome and important and then shoots them down, or blames someone when a seemingly good suggestion does not work out.

One leader, faced with closing down a once-promising avenue of inquiry, called the team together for a "final debrief". In this meeting he praised the project manager for having the courage to close it down, and focused discussion on "what can we learn from this project? How can we apply those learnings to other projects now? To future projects?" He made sure that the "lessons learned" had to do with process and not with personalities. And then he provided pizza and beer — not exactly a celebration, but certainly not a blame-fest. His team went on to new and better projects with renewed energy. This kind of leadership maturity produces the sense of psychological safety that frees employees to be innovative.

This kind of leadership maturity is also important on a day-to-day basis. The leader who fosters innovation must take an interest in the employees and must consistently avoid a harsh or abrupt style of interaction. Any interaction that implies "just do what I say" also implies "don't think". That can be effective in a dire emergency, or when the work itself is well-defined and well-known. It is death to innovation.

Almost as important are questions concerning rules and "bureaucracy". Here the leader has two responsibilities. The first is to ensure that the rules and regulations in place are truly necessary. Unnecessary rules and bureaucracy not only waste time, but they distract employees from more important innovative thoughts. And they create a narrow, unimaginative mindset — the opposite of what you want. Some rules you may be able to simplify or eliminate on your own. Others you may need to challenge with upper management.

The other responsibility is communication: your employees need to understand not only what the rule is, but also why it makes sense. If you can explain the rule sensibly, most often employees will accept it without feeling too constrained.

Flexibility Questions to ask as a leader:

- When someone makes a "strange" suggestion, do I first look for what is good about the idea? Do I recognize and use the good aspects of the idea even if it is not workable in the way that it was offered?
- If I have to say no to an idea, do I take the time to give the employee credit for offering it, to explain the reasoning and the business realities behind my answer, and ask for the employee's help in either working within or working around those limits? (e.g., "Can we find a way to do this — or at least some of it — without a capital investment at this time? Is there another way to approach your idea?")
- Do I model behaviors of openness to new ideas and to learning?
- When we have inevitable rules and limits, do I make the reason for them clear to my team? (It is seemingly *unnecessary* rules that spoil the feeling of Flexibility, not rules that make sense.)
- Equally important: Do I challenge with upper management any rules that I cannot sensibly explain?
- How do I handle disappointments and setbacks? Do I blame the "culprit" or do I take this as an opportunity to learn and improve?

Creating a sense of Flexibility is an obvious starting place for creating an innovative climate. But, by itself, it is not enough. Employees must also feel a sense of personal **Responsibility** for their work; they need to feel that authority has been delegated to them, that they can act in their job without constantly checking with their boss. In other words, they feel that it is acceptable for them to take initiative in their work, to solve problems themselves. When people have a sense of Responsibility, they psychologically "own" the work. Remember the aforementioned six executives who each "owned" the transformation of their business — they each put their heart into making it work, engaging in all sorts of innovative problem-solving along the way.

Responsibility also has two aspects: (1) autonomy, the feeling that one can make decisions without consulting the boss; and (2) risk-taking, the degree to which employees feel encouraged to take calculated risks. Both of these aspects of the experience of Responsibility are central to innovation.

In order to be motivated to think more deeply and creatively about their work, employees need to psychologically "own" their work, to have a sense of autonomy. This is difficult if the boss is constantly interfering, telling the employee *exactly how* something should be done. It is worse yet if the boss, with all good intentions, takes over crucial tasks, indicating that the employee is not to be trusted to do his/her own work properly or on time. At the same time, you do need to show that you are interested in employees' progress and are aware of what they are doing. You can show interest by responding to difficulties with helpful questions, neither taking over the process by supplying answers nor leaving the problem entirely to the employees. This insightful questioning can happen casually: "Have you talked to so-and-so?", "What if you approached it this way?", "Do you need to have someone else do other parts of your work so you can complete this?" This casual, daily "taking an interest" in the employees' work problems can add enormous value, both in terms of motivation and in terms of practical help and resources. You can also do this more formally, in a team setting, by facilitating the process of gathering and examining data and possibilities and building a plan, helping the team work through the problem and come to a plan, rather than deciding for them. This process of bringing the team together to examine data, consider the implications and build a plan to move forward is one of the behaviors we see most consistently in outstanding leaders. It takes more time than just deciding and announcing, but it saves time in moving forward because everyone understands the new plan in detail and feels a personal responsibility to make it work.

Some companies have found that going further with autonomy enhances innovation. 3M and Google have famously allowed their employees certain amounts of time (up to 20%) to work on "whatever interests them" — and have found that often this is the most productive time. The world of IT has, for years, allowed programmers to set their own hours of work, with benefits to productivity.

In addition, employees need to feel that risk-taking centered around "doing something new" is encouraged. This is more than just saying "take reasonable business risks" — it is explaining and acknowledging the kinds of risks and changes that are welcomed. It is making risk-taking around innovation part of your regular business discussion, making clear the kinds and extent of the risks you want to encourage.

Responsibility Questions to ask as a leader:

- Do I accept and encourage employees' decisions *when they are different from the way I would do it* (but the results are acceptable)? Or do I tend to micro-manage, and want to make sure that everything is done just the way I would do it?
- When I am stressed, do I personally take over the most important work (thus sending the message that I do not really trust my employees to do their work well)?
- Do I encourage risk-taking by accepting the fact that "risk" means the new ideas will not always work, that some "failures" are inevitable?
- Am I calm and encouraging when the inevitable disappointments occur? Do I help the team figure out the most useful learnings from these events?
- Do I support the work by taking an interest and asking stimulating questions?
- Do I give my employees as much autonomy as possible?

Team Commitment is based on the employees' feeling that they like and trust their co-workers, and that people help each other to get the job done. It measures the employees' perception that everyone is working toward a common objective, and will exert extra effort when needed.

Team Commitment includes pride in belonging to the organization. If innovation is the result of the "genius working alone", then team commitment would be irrelevant. However, in business, real innovation that actually gets implemented is usually the result of team effort. A recent, unpublished study we conducted showed that even among hard scientists, thought by everyone to be "solitary, eccentric geniuses", the most successful commercial innovations were the result of collaboration. These scientists did work alone most of the time, but they worked best together.

Therefore, Team Commitment is an important component of innovation, as it helps to ensure that people can build on each other's ideas and insights and also serves to mitigate some of the stress and risk of innovation. Innovation is much easier if people feel that "we are in this together" and that others will help implement or pick up some of the slack.

Fostering an innovative team does not mean engaging in a series of "team building" exercises, though you do want to encourage team members to know each other and to get along well. Innovative team commitment has several components: work that is structured so that the team has an important, challenging innovative task to work on together; a sense of psychological safety and emotional support; a practice of robust but respectful discussion and debate of ideas and suggestions, learning from each other and from experience.

First, you want to create clarity about the task and the range of innovation you want as discussed earlier in the chapter. For the best chance of success, be sure that the team's work is challenging, that the task is both clear and important to them, and that it is something the innovative team must work on together to accomplish. Setting the task and the structure of the team is part of your role as a leader (Wageman, Nunes, Burruss and Hackman, 2008).

You want to create a feeling of "psychological safety" and "learning orientation" within the team and with you. You may want to ensure that the team has unstructured, "social" time to get to know each other and develop relationships (especially if you are leading a group of scientists or highly technical professionals). You certainly want to encourage support within the team and discourage within-team competition. Competitiveness can help innovation, but only when it is focused on other teams or other companies. Certainly you want to set an example of treating your team members with respect, and insisting that they do the same with each other. If someone really cannot treat team members with respect, you may need to exclude him/her from the innovative team. Helping the team to have friendly interactions and ensuring that they have the time to build positive relationships pays off in stronger Team Commitment and greater possibilities for collaboration. Including the "whole person" and their outside interests helps the employees to bring those interests and perspectives to work. Doing so may spark a fresh, innovative idea, because innovation often results from two or more different perspectives coming together on a problem or possibility.

To encourage active learning, invite the team to participate in the development of ideas and decisions, acting on the assumption that the employees are intelligent, thoughtful and that their ideas are worth considering seriously. Once you have provided clarity about the task and the parameters, you are likely to hold meetings where you listen more than you speak. This does not mean completely dropping the reins — a well-timed and thoughtful comment or question can clarify an issue or stimulate thinking without dominating the discussion.

To encourage innovation in the team, you are likely to reward the group rather than always singling out individuals, so as to encourage collaboration and team commitment. If you really build Team Commitment, the resulting ideas and accomplishments may indeed be so collaborative that it is most appropriate to recognize the group rather than individuals.

Team Commitment Questions to ask as a leader:

- Do I establish the conditions for my team to work together effectively? Do I structure their work so that they have important innovative tasks that they can only accomplish together?
- How do I use our time together? Do I set up and take the time for discussion of important issues?
- Do I help my team see how their work supports each other, or do I encourage competition within the team? Do I model and insist on candid but respectful discussion?
- When someone has a partly usable idea, do I encourage the team to help develop that idea and make it useful?
- Do my team members know each other as people, not just as workers?

So far, we have discussed four dimensions of organizational climate that support innovation in a fairly straightforward way. They merely need to be adjusted slightly to foster innovation. There are two additional climate dimensions where you may need to radically re-think ordinary management practice in order to support innovation. These are two areas where the practices that support and enhance performance under ordinary circumstances can be counter-productive for innovation. These two areas are also at the core of what many people think of as the traditional tasks and prerogatives of management: setting standards of performance, and doling out rewards (or punishments) for meeting (or not meeting) those standards.

The **Standards** dimension measures the emphasis that employees feel management puts on improving performance, doing one's best, setting challenging but attainable goals and not tolerating mediocrity. Ordinarily a strong emphasis on Standards helps to improve performance, especially when other climate dimensions are also strong.

Standards reflects how strongly you focus employees' attention on key aspects of performance, usually on certain "objective" and clear performance measures. Doing so enhances that performance but "narrows the aperture" for thinking, and can detract from larger innovation. Employees who feel strongly that management encourages performance improvement may be more likely to think of small, incremental, paradigm-consistent improvements. However, there is a danger that over-emphasis on Standards, especially when other climate dimensions are not so strong, can cause employees to avoid risks and avoid innovation (because, in the short run, innovation can distract them from maintaining your performance standards).

If you want "big" paradigm-changing innovation, you may have to significantly change your approach to Standards. Normally, the Standards dimension is about setting goals that are challenging but achievable (basically, doing the same thing a bit better, e.g., "reduce production cost by 5%"). But for moderate to radical innovation, it may be better to set wildly "unachievable" goals (e.g., "make the same product or a product with the same usefulness for 1/10th the cost"). Even if you do not actually achieve the goal, setting such a wild goal helps people think about the situation in a very different way, and may inspire innovations that make deeper changes and bigger performance improvements. Remember the Indian CEO who asked how the bank could serve the very poor villagers and not lose money in the process? This was a wild goal, not the normal standard of performance at all, and it "broke set" and set people's imaginations loose to come up with a new business model (Prahalad, 2009; Spencer *et al.*, 2007).

For paradigm-changing innovation, you may also have to relax your ordinary performance standards, at least when and for those people who are actively involved in innovating. It is often impossible for the same person to simultaneously maintain the absolutely highest performance standards in the old paradigm and create a significantly new paradigm. The same people who were designing the new village cooperatives were certainly not also running a normal branch office to maximum efficiency. So the performance standards for people engaged in innovation need to realistically reflect their innovative work, and perhaps include certain milestones of progress in innovation instead of the normal performance standard.

Innovation, especially significant innovation, is more likely to thrive with BHAGs — "Big, Hairy Audacious Goals" (Collins and Porras, 1996) — and less concern about whether you make every last bit of that goal than with moderate goals and an emphasis on precise measurement against the goal. So, if you have a culture of strong Standards, you may need to re-think and re-tune your approach to setting standards — the more so the bigger the innovation you want. You may even want to change your approach to Standards radically, as David Farr did at Emerson. Instead of continuing detailed operations reviews (traditional high Standards), he simply asks, "What are you/your group doing that is new?" and if the answer is "Not much", he follows up with "How much more money are you making?"

Standards Questions to ask as a leader:

- Am I setting goals in a way that is consistent with the type of innovation I want to achieve?
- Am I setting challenging but realistic goals for the "incremental" or "paradigm-consistent" innovations my team must achieve?
- Are my standards and goals "open-ended" enough to encourage innovation that is "paradigm-breaking"? Am I using BHAGs when appropriate?
- Are the measures of progress or success appropriate for the innovation we want and need?

Rewards is the trickiest aspect of management for innovation. One of the most robust and often repeated findings in social science is that extrinsic rewards (e.g., promising bonuses, prizes, pay raises and so on for performance) *detract* from innovative problem-solving (Amabile, 1998; Woodman, Sawyer and Griffin, 1993). Extrinsic rewards work fine when both the task and exactly how to accomplish it are very clear. And they work rather well for many sales roles. This is why "carrot and stick" management has been so popular. But, once you need people to "think outside the box" at all, extrinsic rewards can actually be *counterproductive.*

This finding applies to all pre-announced incentive schemes, all the "prizes" that the employee is likely to anticipate. It does not apply to what you do "after-the-fact" and it does not apply to "intrinsic" rewards such as interesting challenges and the time taken to pursue them. Does this mean that pay does not matter at all? No, it is still important to pay employees fairly — if they are really underpaid, the best people are likely to be recruited away from you. But, it does mean you have a number of other ways to reward and recognize your best people that do not cost as much and are also likely to encourage further innovation (Amabile, 1998; Amabile and Fisher, 2009).

You may not have control over your company's incentive scheme, and there may be other good reasons for various incentive or variable pay schemes, but do not rely on these to motivate innovation. If your company has an incentive or variable pay system, you can communicate it in a quiet, matter-of-fact way and then pay more attention to other ways to recognize people's contributions.

So, as a manager, what can you actively do to motivate your employees for innovation? First, we need to think about what innovators really want, what is *intrinsically* rewarding to them. While you should be able to notice what matters most to the people who work with you, here are some general observations. Innovators enjoy interesting challenges and the autonomy, freedom, and time to pursue them. They like recognition for their innovation and for their role in it, not just from you but also from their peers and customers. They like seeing their innovation have a positive impact on the business and on the world. They like the opportunity to learn and grow.

In a recent, unpublished Hay Group study of innovative scientists, the scientists were insistent on telling us how upset they were when they and their contributions were not personally recognized by management. They were also unhappy when denied the opportunity to go to conferences that they felt were important to their work, or where they would be recognized. Every second your people spend in thinking, talking or being upset about such negative interactions is time that they are *not* thinking productively about their work. Skip-level recognition can be even more powerful than recognition by one's direct manager, so be sure to personally recognize not only your direct reports, but also those who are a level or two lower in the organization. And, involve your own manager in recognizing the innovators in your group.

When the Rewards dimension of organizational climate is high, people feel that they are recognized and rewarded for innovative work. They know where they stand in terms of their performance and feel that recognition is given to excellent innovative performance in contrast to ordinary performance. They see their good ideas put to work and their contribution is acknowledged. To make sure that this dimension of your climate supports innovation, you will want to make sure that you give recognition and encouragement for contributing new ideas (even if they are not used in the end) and for effort and progress on realizing a new idea not just for profitable results. You also want to ensure that everyone involved in a successful innovation is acknowledged, not just those who were active at the end of the project.

Especially, recognition needs to be given to those who have the insight and courage to end a pet project that is not working out and to redirect energy elsewhere. It is too easy to hang on to ideas way too long, either out of attachment to the idea or out of fear of admitting "failure". Paradoxically, the "failure" of a seemingly good idea needs to be recognized and "rewarded" so as to: (1) encourage others to try new ideas without fear of failure; and (2) redirect energy elsewhere with a satisfactory "closure".

Innovative work can also be "rewarded" with the opportunity to do more innovative work — with the time and freedom to work on interesting problems. The opportunity to learn and to network with other people working on related questions can also be rewarding. Attending conferences and conventions or setting up mini-conferences within your company or with your suppliers and customers can be rewarding in several ways. These events provide an opportunity for innovative work to be recognized and applauded, not only by you, but also by others. They also provide an opportunity for making connections for future work, and for learning or being inspired by what other people are doing. They provide an opportunity for making connections with customers and suppliers, focused on innovations to meet their needs.

Rewards Questions to ask as a leader:

- Do I recognize new ideas and suggestions of my team?
- How do I provide feedback and encouragement to my team's innovative efforts? How regularly?
- How do I handle setbacks and mistakes? Do I punish team members who make mistakes?
- Does the reward system facilitate or inhibit innovation? Do I overly focus my team on external rewards?
- Do I know what non-financial rewards my team finds most motivating? Do I link these intrinsic rewards to innovation?

---

6. Summary of Organizational Climate

There is evidence that innovation is particularly susceptible to shifts in organizational climate; other aspects of performance are comparatively robust, but innovative thinking shrivels up quickly when the organizational weather is dry or chilly. For example, Amabile (2006) found that the impact of an unpleasant interaction with one's boss inhibits innovative thinking for a much longer time than it does other aspects of performance. So, the first order of business is to create a positive work environment. But, you can go beyond that to create a positive work environment that is specifically tuned to support the kinds of innovation you desire. Incremental, paradigm-consistent innovation needs more Clarity about where the limits of the paradigm are (e.g., "we are not going to become....; we do want to find new ways to be more....."). The risks are lower (though the rewards are also lower), so this kind of innovation is closer to everyday "excellent operations" or continuous improvement. Radical, paradigm-breaking innovation needs more support through all the climate dimensions, particularly Clarity, Standards and Rewards, where progress, new ideas, and the courage to stop pursuing something that is not working at all need to be recognized as real contributions.

7. Putting the Framework into Practice

As a leader, how can you create an organizational climate that will drive the innovative outcomes that will move your organization forward? What leadership behaviors will you need to focus on and change? How will you implement the necessary changes and stay on track? Most importantly, how will you know your efforts are working? The guidelines below will help you focus your efforts and create an organizational climate where innovation can flourish.

Step 1: Determine the Type of Innovation You Want to Achieve

As a leader, are you focused on increasing efficiency and reducing costs? Are you concerned with improving your existing product line or enhancing the experience of your current customers? These types of paradigm-consistent innovations will require you to focus on certain aspects of organizational climate over others and will also determine the types of leadership behaviors you will need to zero in on to create the right climate for the innovation. If you desire more radical innovation that is potentially "paradigm-breaking", then you will need to focus differently on the climate dimensions as we have discussed in this chapter. The bottom line is that you will need to clearly define and articulate the type of innovation you want to achieve as a first step in order to optimize the use of our framework. What is your innovation objective? Once you have determined the answer to that question, you can use this chapter to focus on the ways you will need to adapt your behavior and the climate you create to support the innovation you need.

Step 2: Identify the Climate Dimensions that May Be Blocking Your Employees' Innovations

Taking action as leader to improve organizational climate requires an understanding of which of the six climate dimensions may be hampering your team's innovation efforts. As a leader, you need to conduct an assessment to make sure the actions you take will truly help to focus your efforts in the right direction and facilitate necessary improvements. Survey-based climate measures are available for this purpose and are preferred in order to accurately pinpoint climate strengths and opportunities for improvement. A less formal but viable alternative approach is to begin asking the right questions of your team to establish an ongoing dialogue about the climate they experience and the adjustments that are needed.

In order to accomplish this, you can use the questions offered throughout this chapter to gauge your team's experience and discuss the dimensions of organizational climate that are helping them to be more innovative and those that are detracting from their innovative efforts. As a rule of thumb, the greater the number of questions answered affirmatively for a given climate dimension, the more positive the team experience with respect to that aspect of climate tends to be. Discussion along these lines can focus on how to maintain and improve the good things already in place. When you begin to hear a large number of "no" responses to questions related to a particular climate dimension, this suggests an opportunity for improvement. Dialogue with the team should focus on ways to change and improve the climate in that particular area.

A simplified set of "starter" questions for each dimension of organizational climate is provided below. We have found that starting with a small number of key questions for each dimension helps to get the ball rolling with teams and can foster an ongoing dialogue about the climate for innovation. As your team discussions progress, you can use the additional questions provided in the chapter for each of the climate dimensions.

How is our climate for innovation? Some "start-up" questions to use with your team.

Ask your team to provide feedback on the following items using the response scale below.
Response scale: True, False, Not Sure

Clarity: I understand the innovations we are trying to achieve and why they are important.
Flexibility: New ideas are welcomed here.

> **Responsibility:** I am encouraged to take reasonable risks and try new things.
> **Team Commitment:** When it comes to innovation, we are all working toward common goals.
> **Standards:** Our goals make sense with respect to the innovations we are trying to achieve.
> **Rewards:** I receive feedback and recognition for my innovative efforts on a regular basis.

Step 3: Create a Change Plan

Once you have identified the organizational climate dimensions that you will need to develop and change, create a specific development plan to help you stay focused. A good plan should include specific objectives (e.g., "Improve team members' understanding of marketing innovation goals until they can each express them accurately in their own words and bring in an innovative suggestion that could fit those goals"; or "Delegate responsibility for cost-reduction strategy development to ———, check in, offer support, but do not micro-manage her"). Each objective should have a corresponding completion date.

You should also indicate as clearly as possible the leadership behaviors, or changes in structure or procedures, associated with each objective and how you will measure progress. You will also need a way to evaluate the effectiveness of your change efforts. How will you know whether the new leadership behaviors you are trying to perfect are working? You will definitely need feedback from others as you execute your plan. Will you ask your team members to give you feedback on the changes? Can an external coach or peer manager "shadow" you at a few meetings and provide feedback on your efforts? You will need to identify individuals in your business environment who can provide periodic feedback and help you to stay focused and personally accountable for the results of your plan. The most important feedback is the changes in your team's behavior. You might want to look for things like: for increased Team Commitment, "Do my team members support and encourage each other more with less sniping and criticizing?" or for increased Responsibility, "Do my team members solve more problems on their own, or bring me more suggested solutions and fewer requests for me to solve their problems?" To use this kind of measure, you need to establish some sort of baseline for comparison, e.g., "Now I get about two requests a week that people really should be able to handle on their own". Ultimately, the measure of your leadership and climate improvement efforts is whether your team produces more or better innovations than they did before (and, most likely, whether there are clear indications that they are happier and more productive as well).

8. Conclusion

We believe that innovation will be critically important to the future growth success of organizations. Ultimately, innovation, whether paradigm-consistent or paradigm-breaking, will only happen if the right climate is established and the leadership behaviors required to realize that climate are put into action and demonstrated consistently and effectively. We hope that this brief chapter will help enable leaders to develop and enhance their ability to lead innovation and foster the type of organizational climate where innovation, growth and long-term business success can occur.

References

Amabile, T. M. (1998). How to Kill Creativity. *Harvard Business Review*, 76(5): 76–87.

Amabile, T. M. (2006). Sweat the Small Stuff. *New Business* (Spring Issue).

Amabile, T. M. and Fisher, C. M. (2009). Stimulate Creativity by Fueling Passion. *Blackwell Handbook of Principles of Organizational Behavior*, 2nd Edition. London: Wiley-Blackwell.

Andrew, J. P., Haanaes, K., Michael, D. C., Sirkin, H. L. and Taylor, A. (2007). *Innovation 2007: A BCG Senior Management Survey*. Boston Consulting Group.

Andrew, J. P., Haanaes, K., Michael, D. C., Sirkin, H. L. and Taylor, A. (2008). *Innovation 2008: Is the Tide Turning?* Boston Consulting Group.

Andrew, J. P., Haanaes, K., Michael, D. C., Sirkin, H. L. and Taylor, A. (2009). *Innovation 2009: Making Hard Decisions in the Downturn*. Boston Consulting Group.

Andrew, J. P., Manget, J., Michael, D. C., Taylor, A. and Zablit, H. (2010). *Innovation 2010: A Return to Prominence and the Emergence of a New World Order*. Boston Consulting Group.

Collins, J. and Porras, J. (1996). Building Your Company's Vision. *Harvard Business Review*, 74(5): 65–77.

Edmondson, A. (1999). Psychological Safety and Learning Behavior in Work Teams. *Administrative Science Quarterly*, 44(2): 350–383.

Gardner, H. (1993). *Creating Minds: An Anatomy of Creativity As Seen Through the Lives of Freud, Einstein, Picasso, Stravinsky, Eliot, Graham and Gandhi.* New York: Basic Books.

Goleman, D. (2000). Leadership That Gets Results. *Harvard Business Review*, 78(2): 78–90.

Hay Group (2008). *Organizational Climate Technical Manual.*

Hay Group (2009). Unpublished study.

Kirton, M. (1994). *Adaptors and Innovators: Styles of Creativity and Problem Solving.* London: Routledge.

Prahalad, C. K. (2009). *Fortune at the Bottom of the Pyramid.* New Jersey: Wharton School Publishing.

Spencer, S., Rajah, T., Narayan, S. A., Mohan, S. and Lahiri, G. (2007). *The Indian CEO: A Portrait of Excellence.* New Delhi: Response Books (Sage).

The World's Most Admired Companies: The 50 All-Stars (2012, March 19). *Fortune*, 165(4): 139–140.

Wageman, R., Nunes, D., Burruss, J. and Hackman, R. (2008). *Senior Leadership Teams: What It Takes to Make Them Great.* Boston, MA: Harvard Business School Press.

Woodman, R. W., Sawyer, J. E. and Griffin, R. W. (1993). Toward a Theory of Organizational Creativity. *Academy of Management Review*, 18(2): 293–321.

Chapter 6

Unblocking Innovation:
Breaking the Shackle of Assumptions

Samuel Chun

Executive Director, Olin Management Solutions,
Olin Business School, Washington University in St. Louis

Anjan V. Thakor

John E. Simon Professor of Finance and Director of the WFA Center
for Finance and Accounting Research and Doctoral Program,
Olin Business School, Washington University in St. Louis

This chapter introduces a new approach to innovation, based on identifying the key assumptions in the prevailing business model of the firm or the industry and discarding a few key assumptions supporting the existing business model that are widely accepted within the industry. The idea is that every business model has a set of explicit and implicit assumptions based on which the model is constructed. These assumptions often have to do with consumer preferences for various product/service attributes, the demand for the product/service at any given price, the nature of the value chain from production to the ultimate distribution of the product/service to the consumer, and so on. Often, these assumptions are supported by experience or historical data. The key to innovation is to identify which of these assumptions can be discarded or replaced with new assumptions, so that a novel business model emerges, and this model leads to spectacular new growth. This chapter discusses how an organization can systematically approach innovation this way and provides numerous examples of instances in which this approach has been successfully implemented.

1. Introduction

Innovation is the Holy Grail for those in pursuit of enhanced value creation. To those interested in studying people and organizations, innovation energizes the organization and "liberates" people from staid, in-the-box thinking. To the marketing expert, innovation creates new products and services with possibly new channels of distribution. To the economist, innovation is a mechanism for generating super-normal profits. To the finance expert, innovation is often a path to higher shareholder returns. But what is the secret of successful innovation?

In this chapter, we focus on a particular approach to innovation that can be practiced by any individual or organization. The basic premise of this approach is that innovation requires making something new that is better, and what it replaces is predicated on a particular set of *assumptions* about the environment. What exists today is probably the best product or service if one takes the underlying set of assumptions on which it is based as a given. So if one continues to take those assumptions as fixed, it is difficult to visualize how one can come up with an innovation that is better than what exists already. To innovate, one must first *discard* an assumption that is important for the existing product or service and replace it with something else that will lead the product/service design down an entirely different path. The assumption that is discarded must be important — even pivotal — for the existing product or service in that it is widely shared within the industry and thus has empirical support. Discarding such an assumption therefore means that the innovator is going *against* current wisdom. And going against the current wisdom frees the innovator to delve into areas, combine and recombine components and ideas, and branch into areas previously assumed to be "off limits."

In what follows, we first describe the approach in more detail in Section 2. Then we provide two case studies to illustrate the concept — the invention of the airplane (Section 3) and the invention of the iPod (Section 4). Section 5 presents a summary of how one can operationalize this principle for any innovation, while Section 6 concludes.

2. More on the "Unblocking" Approach

Every product, service and business model that we see is based on a set of assumptions about the environment, including assumptions about customers, suppliers, competitors, geopolitics, the government, demographics, weather patterns, and so on. Given these assumptions, firms and individuals optimize and come up with designs for products, services and business models. We only see the output of this process — the actual products, services and business models — but those involved in producing these use the underlying assumptions that may not be visible to others. Often these assumptions are not even explicitly articulated by those involved in the production process, but they nonetheless dominate how these producers go about designing their products and services.

Consider the example of the US coffee industry in the early 1980s. The industry was dominated by three firms — Nestlé, Proctor & Gamble and General Foods — that collectively had over 90% market share. Coffee was a commodity, and profit margins were compressed by intense competition to sell to highly price-conscious customers. The major players were engaged in a fierce battle for market share, but no one was making profits, let alone generating enough profits to exceed the cost of capital and create value.

What were the key assumptions the major players were relying on in the coffee business? Here are a few:

(1) Coffee is a commodity and the consumer cares only about price.
(2) To compete effectively, you need to be the lowest-cost producer, which requires maximizing scale, which in turn requires winning the war for market share.
(3) The market for coffee is largely undifferentiated and consists of the entire grocery-shopping public.

These assumptions were the foundation of the business model that all the major coffee manufacturers were using in the early 1980s. Each of these assumptions had strong empirical support. There seemed to be no reason for any of the players to seriously challenge any of these assumptions.

Enter Starbucks. It challenged and discarded all three assumptions. By using Arabica coffee beans instead of the cheaper Robusta beans and by charging customers almost $2 for a cup of coffee, Starbucks discarded Assumptions 1 and 2. And by focusing on selling through cafés located near places of work and thereby appealing primarily to an upwardly mobile professional customer base, Starbucks discarded Assumption 3.

Why did Starbucks' unblocking strategy work? The reason is that each of the three assumptions was valid on its own and it was difficult to discard any one of them while accepting the others. Starbucks discarded all three of them. Instead of trying to serve the whole market through grocery stores — as the major coffee manufacturers were doing — Starbucks chose to initially serve a select subset of the market through cafés, focusing on the entire coffee consumption experience of the customer rather than only on selling coffee.

The message is clear. New products and services emerge from someone discarding the assumptions that dominate the existing paradigm. The challenge is deciding which assumptions to discard.

3. The Case of Airplanes

Introduction

Sadi Carnot laid the foundations for a simple 2-stroke reciprocating internal combustion engine in 1824. Samuel Morey secured a patent for a working version of the Carnot engine in 1826. Because of Daniel Bernoulli, the principle of aerodynamic lift was well-understood by the mid-1700s. Archimedes' screw provided hints of propeller technology circa 250 BC. Kites were used for flight in early Chinese history. Yet, fully controlled flight did not occur until 1905. Since then, the progress has been relatively swift. What breakthroughs pushed flight to the forefront of commercial transportation, and which key assumptions were let go to unleash the potential of manned flight?

Background

Manned flight has a long history. While we can point to ancient mythology such as Daedalus and Icarus as idealizations, examples of attempted execution of manned flight can be found in the historical artifacts of China dating as far back as the 6th century AD. Abbas Ibn Firnas (Andalusia) demonstrated the first hang glider in the 9th century AD, as did Jack Toff (Greece) in the same era. Leonardo da Vinci (15th century) expressed several visions of flight, which were captured in his various illustrations, but executed none of these. Hot air balloons became serious objects of air exploration in the late 18th century, and Daniel Bernoulli published his fluid equation, which describes the process of aerodynamic lift, around 1737.

Starting with the fundamental observation that solid objects are heavier than air, yet many solid objects fly (insects and birds), it took much experimentation and many years of trial and error before powered flight was invented.

Brief Historical Sections

Kites

General Gao Huan took over the Chinese province of Northern Qi upon the death of Emperor Yuan Lang. Upon Gao Huan's death, Huan's son, Gao Yang assumed control and subsequently imprisoned Yuan Lang's son, Yuan Huangtou, who was the emperor apparent. Gao Yang quite literally launched the incumbent emperor Yuan Huangtou on his short career as one of the first experimental human test pilots for a large kite which was tossed off of the high tower of Ye. While Huangtou survived the flight, thus marking the kite's aerodynamic success, he was executed by Yang shortly thereafter.

Spain became the next proving ground for kites. Muslim engineer Abbas Ibn Firnas continued the tradition of tossing oneself off of high buildings by jumping off the minaret of the great mosque at Cordoba in 852 while attached to a device resembling a parachute. Firnas built the device using wood and stiffened cloth, which he would improve over the next decades of his life. Though Firnas' first series of inventions functioned more as drag-inducing mechanisms that slowed rapid descent to a survivable level, later versions comprised actual wings that allowed the wearer to glide for sustained periods of time. These later innovations laid the foundations for Eilmer of Malmesbury, who managed to successfully glide approximately 200 meters around the year 1010 AD.

George Cayley began a systematic physical analysis of flight towards the end of the 18th century. His basic aerodynamic principles and terminology (such as lift and drag) have survived the passage of time and technology.

Balloons

Most flying inventions before hot air balloons focused on descent-based flight, exploiting air currents and flow to sustain a body against gravity.

Ballooning, which became a popular pastime in late 18th century Europe, was all about lift by using heated air to defy gravity.

While not steerable, balloons offered the first opportunity for prolonged, manned flight. In 1783, de Rozier and d'Arlandes traveled approximately five miles in a hot air balloon powered by wood fire. The steerable version of the balloon was the dirigible. Using steam power, Henri Giffard managed a controlled, 15-mile flight in 1852. The first fully controllable "airship" was the La France dirigible. The La France was invented by Charles Renard and Arthur Krebs for the French army, and was capable of flying 12–15 miles per hour using a small electric motor. While many successes marked the history of balloons and dirigibles, most of these inventions were fragile and unreliable for repeated use and general passenger transport.

Fixed wing aircraft

Manned flight exploiting aerodynamic principles began gaining momentum in the mid-19th century. This time period saw inventors such as Jean-Marie Bris, Felix du Temple, Herbert Wenham, Otto Lilienthal, Percy Pilcher and Octave Chanute. Wenham created the world's first wind-tunnel to test new wing designs in 1871, further refining aerofoil understanding and technology.

Experimentation in the field of flight was not a riskless endeavor. After approximately 2,500 successful flights, Lilienthal's last craft suffered a broken wing mid-flight, causing him to fall from approximately 60 feet in the air. He died the following day, muttering "sacrifices must be made…" However, through his many experiments, Lilienthal realized that power was a key link and he had been working on light engines that could propel his crafts.

Samuel Pierpont Langley achieved engine-powered flights of 3,000 feet in 1896 with his Aerodrome #5. Later that same year, his Aerodrome #6 achieved a powered flight of over 4,500 feet. Langley's Aerodromes were non-steerable, unmanned craft, which were launched via catapult from atop of a houseboat on the Potomac River, near Quantico, Virginia. The Aerodromes had no landing gear (to save weight) and could attain speeds of approximately 25 miles per hour.

Like Lilienthal, Langley realized that power was key to sustained flight. He obtained funding to pursue his engine designs. From 1901–1902, seeking even more power, Langley and his colleague/contractor Steven Balzer designed a 52-horsepower engine to drive his Aerodrome. Having now both a plane and a power platform, Langley combined the two but found that his aircraft were too fragile for the amount of power created by his engine designs. Concurrent with and independent of Langley's efforts, the brothers Orville and Wilbur Wright created their own versions of gliders at the beginning of the 20th century. Like prior attempts at flying, the Wrights incorporated various wing cross-sections and on-board power to propel their craft. However, unlike prior designs by other inventors, the Wrights had incorporated controls that allowed their airplane to roll the wings up or down on either side, pitch the nose down or up, and yaw the plane left or right. Thus, the plane could effectively navigate its air space in three dimensions.

The Wright brothers, therefore, are generally credited as the first to execute sustained, self-powered and controlled heavier-than-air flight. The Wright Company built many evolutions of its original model, 19 in all. The later versions, ending with the Model L, were very much in line with the fighter biplanes used in World War I.

Assumptions

While the history of manned flight yields abundant examples of invention, ingenuity and outright genius, it also portrays a string of assumptions that were systematically dropped as progress was made in flight technology. Below is a list of the popular assumptions prevailing at that time:

- Flight exploits drag (Kites).
- Flight relies on human power.
- Flight requires lighter-than-air gases (Balloons).
- Wings must be rigid.
- Aerofoil principles apply only to wings (Propellers use this same property to generate thrust).

We can combine all of these assumptions into one single overarching assumption that impeded the invention of airplanes, and it is that heavier-than-air flying machines (that do not just rely on drag or use human power or lighter-than-air gases for elevation) are simply not possible. For example, the much-heralded Irish physicist, Lord Kelvin, is credited with making the famous statement, "Heavier-than-air flying machines are impossible."

The Wright brothers clearly dropped this assumption, and in fact made the opposite assumption, namely that flying machines were a reality waiting to be discovered! They then focused their efforts on how to make it happen. This led to the realization that there were two key problems that needed to be simultaneously attacked — navigation and power.

On the issue of navigation, the challenge was to come up with a way to control the airplane. While the Wrights contributed much to our modern understanding of wing cross-section, lift and drag, one of their key contributions to manned flight came from the simpler question of how to control the airplane. During the development of their glider prototypes, the Wright brothers determined that the wings and fins of their Flyer needed to move in new ways if their craft were to be controllable in three dimensions.

For the craft to ascend, steer and descend safely, they invented three devices to serve three distinct purposes. First, the Wrights added an "elevator" in front of the pilot to provide a way to pitch the nose of the craft up and down during flight. This extension also added balance and leverage to the front end of the Flyer. Second, they invented a way of warping the wings during flight to allow the wings to "roll." While this worked to some degree in helping to steer the plane, the Flyer tended to "skip" in turns. To remedy this, a rudder replaced the original fixed tail which forced the nose of the craft to yaw left and right, thus better enabling turns by reducing rear drag, and allowing for less wing deformation, which sometimes had the unfortunate consequence of reducing wing lift. The combination of flexible wings and rear rudder allowed their Flyer to effectively "bank" turns. The front elevator helped the pilot point the plane up or down for controlled takeoffs and landings. The "wing-warping," rear rudder and the front-mounted elevator in combination effectively solved the problem of control. These three elements remain virtually unchanged in principle in modern aircraft.

As for the issue of power, prior to the Wrights, power for flights was generated through catapults, springs, carbonic acid, compressed air, steam engines and ski ramps. None of these approaches were acceptable to the Wright brothers. So they turned to propellers as the way to generate power for flight, using aerofoil principles in this development. The Wrights converted their understanding of aerodynamic lift and wing shape, and applied their knowledge to propeller design. By some estimates, their propeller design is between 90% and 95% as efficient as modern propeller designs, which is quite astonishing. In the same way a wing produces upward lift by virtue of its bowed shape, a spinning propeller situated properly creates forward "lift" by spinning two mini-wings attached at a center point. This greatly magnifies the ability of an engine to create forward (or backward) motion. Prior to the Wright brothers, there existed virtually no systematic research on propeller design.

Military applications of airplanes and the commercialization of air travel stemmed directly from the Wright brothers' ability to let go of key assumptions regarding wing/fin flexibility and forward propulsion.

What do we learn from this case study of aviation innovation which has so profoundly transformed human ability to transport, explore, trade and develop? First, it was essential for those at the vanguard of the efforts to develop a tool for aviation to drop the limiting assumption that flying machines that weighed more than air were simply impossible. It is worth noting that this was a very plausible assumption, given the state of knowledge that existed in the 18th and 19th centuries. In fact, there was apparently ample empirical evidence available to support this assumption — after all, we did not see any heavier-than-air flying machines buzzing through the skies, and anyone who tried elevating in such a machine had been rudely reminded of the laws of gravity! But it was an assumption nonetheless; there was no theorem in physics which ruled it out. This is the principle of "Primary Assumption Dispensing" — a big assumption must be first dropped in order to get a fundamentally fresh look at the problem. Second, once the initial big assumption was dropped, there were many smaller assumptions that guided the early explorations, such as flight exploits drag, flight depends on human power, etc., which also had to be dispensed with in order to make progress. This is the principle of "Secondary Assumption Dispensing." Quite often, the innovations that result from dropping the initial big assumption are crude and possibly not even commercially feasible, or even if they are feasible they do not represent a profitable opportunity for anyone. In these typical cases, a second wave of refining innovations has to occur in order to sustain and accelerate innovation progress. This wave requires many to engage in Secondary Assumption Dispensing. What is common to both stages of innovation is that the assumptions that were dropped were simply assumptions, and not facts, but they had taken on the appearance of facts.

It is no different in business. Every business faces innovation opportunities that result from Primary and Secondary Assumption Dispensing. For example, most businesses assume that the Law of Downward-Sloping Demand Curves applies to their business, which means that raising price will generally diminish demand. Yet, there are many types of products — economists call them "status goods" — for which a decrease in price could lead to a decrease in demand because, by attracting more buyers who can now afford the product, the good loses the "exclusivity" that attracted a certain group of buyers in the first place. So even an assumption as seemingly basic as higher price means lower demand may not be a good assumption. Look around you for all the assumptions that determine your strategy and drive your business model. Ask yourself: (1) How similar are these assumptions making you to your competitors? (2) Which of these assumptions are limiting innovation in your organization? (3) What alternative assumptions could you make? (4) What new opportunities might present themselves if you made these alternative assumptions?

4. The Apple iPod

Introduction

Amelio told us: "Apple is a boat. There's a hole in the boat and it's taking on water. But there's also a treasure on board. And the problem is, everyone on board is rowing in different directions, so the boat is just standing still. My job is to get everyone rowing in the same direction so we can save the treasure." After he turned away, I looked at the person next to me and asked, "But what about the hole?"[1]

The above anecdote recounts one Silicon Valley CEO's account of an encounter with Apple's then CEO Gil Amelio in 1997, just prior to Steven Jobs' return to Apple Computer, the company he co-founded with Steve Wozniak on April Fool's Day of 1976. The "hole" to which Amelio referred was Apple's losing battle in the personal computer (PC) market to Microsoft Windows-based machines. Some facts:

- Apple's net sales went from a high of $9.8 billion in 1996 to $5.9 billion in 1998.
- Apple's market share of the worldwide PC market went from 16% in 1980 to 3% in 1998.
- Apple's corporate gross margin was approximately 25% throughout the 1990s.
- The average selling price of PCs was decreasing by about 5% per annum.

To plug the "hole" upon returning to Apple, Jobs forged a partnership with software rival Microsoft to launch an Apple version of the industry-dominant "Office" suite, terminated licensing agreements for "Mac-clone" production, created a new line of Internet-ready iMac computers based on fresh industrial design at competitive price points, shut down the flailing "Newton" division of handheld computers, shifted away from Motorola processors to Intel, created Apple's first server software OS X, re-established Apple in the notebook computer arena with the iBook, and entered the retail industry with the Apple Store. Jobs also launched the iPod MP3 music player.

While much of Jobs' efforts focused on shoring up the Mac line of computers in a highly competitive PC market in which Windows was the dominant platform, he also focused on shifting Apple away from its reliance on the PC market as the principal driver of revenue. Indeed, by 2005, net sales of iPod and related products were $13.9 billion, while Macintosh PC sales were $6.2 billion.

---

[1] Brent Schlender, "Something's Rotten in Cupertino," *Fortune*, March 3, 1997.

Some Background: What is an iPod?

Launched approximately 1.5 months after the events of September 11, 2001 at a price of $399, the first iPod was basically a small, high-capacity hard drive controlled by a large, circular button array. Operating software, a small LCD screen and headphones rounded out the package, which played back digitally stored music.

On one level, the iPod was a highly simplified computer that had only one functional capability: to play music. Thus, it was very much in the realm of Apple's traditional core competence from a product development standpoint.

On another level, the iPod embodied a drastic departure from Apple's core business line in that much of the product's success hinged on the company's ability to supply a convenient and cheap way of linking music content from a PC into the iPod. Apple's traditional content was software applications. The iPod required Apple to get into the music distribution business.

From the viewpoint of technology, the iPod was seldom touted as a spectacular technological advance. The iPod hitchhiked on many different systems that were already in existence. By most accounts, the key element that laid the foundations of the music player's success was the link through the iTunes software, which gave consumers an access point to purchase new music both conveniently and inexpensively.

The success of iTunes relied on music publishers' willingness to sell their songs through the Apple platform. The value added to the music industry was a mechanism which would allow for an adequate capture rate of royalties from music sales, which were under threat by software systems such as Napster.

Thus, through the iPod–iTunes combination, Apple had created a system in which the user was linked to the computer which was, in turn, linked to a store that sold music, which Apple managed at marginal economics. According to Jobs:

> "The dirty little secret of all this is there's no way to make money on these stores," he says. For every 99 cents Apple gets from your credit card, 65 cents goes straight to the music label. Another quarter or so gets eaten up by distribution costs. At most, Jobs is left with a dime per track, so even $500 million in annual sales would generate at most $50 million in EBITDA.

Why even bother? "Because we're selling iPods," Jobs says, grinning. That may make iTunes the most benign-looking Trojan horse in software history.[2]

Going a little deeper, in 2006 a 2GB iPod Nano retailed at $199. The bill of materials, or cost, on that model was approximately $90, leaving an approximate gross margin of 55%. Apple's historical business gross margin ranged from 20%–30% in comparison.[3] By the end of 2005, the iPod accounted for 75% of the US market share for portable music players and Apple had sold approximately 42 million iPods.[4]

The Portable Music Player Industry

The first mass-produced MP3-based digital audio player was created in 1997 by SaeHan Information Systems of South Korea. The product, called the "MPMan," was introduced in the spring of 1998. Generally, while the portable music player market was dominated in the 1980s and early 1990s by Sony's ubiquitous "Walkman" tape and CD players, such a clear and dominant leader in the MP3 market was not obvious in the late 1990s.

Apple Computer and Music: What Key Assumption was Abandoned?

If Apple (and Jobs) had merely viewed itself as a computer company, the iPod would likely never have happened. And even if it did, it is difficult to conceive how it could have attained its current levels of success without the (admittedly marginal) music side of the business. Thus, getting into the music business was a critical move for Jobs and Apple.

Apple, like others in the industry, operated under the following implicit or explicit assumptions:

(1) Apple is in the PC industry and its customers are computer users. Thus, Apple's innovation efforts should focus on innovations in the look, feel and functionality of computers.

---

[2]Chris Taylor, "The 99 cent Solution," Time Inc., 2003.
[3]David Yoffie and Yusi Wang, "Apple Computer, 2006," Harvard Business School Press, 2006.
[4]Ina Fried, "Apple Seeks 'Tax' on iPod Accessories," CNET News.com, March 16, 2006.

(2) Apple's main competence is the ability to develop software and its primary challenge is to gain market share in the PC industry by improving efficiency and lowering cost.

(3) Selling music is part of the music industry. There was no example of profitable convergence between the music and PC industries, and indeed the music industry had viewed the emergence of the Internet as a threat to its profit model because of the ease with which music files could be shared by users across the Internet.

Which key assumption did Apple abandon to develop the iPod? The answer, perhaps a bit surprisingly, is Assumption 1 (even though Assumption 3 seems like a tempting low-hanging fruit). To see this, note that PC makers, like most other manufacturers, see their customers as purchasers of their products, i.e., PCs. This then defines the scope of their innovation efforts as being confined to the product they are selling, which for Apple was its Macintosh PC. This is no different from a car manufacturer viewing its customers as car buyers and hence focusing its innovation efforts on the cars themselves, or a company that makes automobile tyres viewing its customers as car manufacturers and hence focusing its innovation on tyres.

But what if the manufacturer focused its innovation efforts not on its product itself, but on *how someone might use the product*? That is, rather than leaving the use of the product to the customer, the manufacturer can innovate on the uses that the *customers* can put the product to. This mind-set opens up a continent of new opportunities for the manufacturer. The reason is simple. For most products, the really big market is not in the initial, intended application of the product. Rather, it lies in the initially unexpected secondary and tertiary applications of the product. For example, the inventor of flat screen monitors probably never imagined the huge market that emerged when the technology was used for television screens.

In a sense, there are some companies that have a business model built around the premise of innovating on customer applications of a known technology. For example, W.L. Gore has a portfolio of technologies that it owns, and its innovation efforts are aimed at developing an increasing array of products that use these technologies. But very few companies define their innovation efforts this way, because most adopt some analog of Assumption 1.

What Apple did was to creatively drop Assumption 1. So rather than leaving the task of coming up with new uses of computing technology to its customers, Apple asked itself: what uses can this technology be put to that may be profitable, given current trends in preferences among consumers at large, rather than just PC users? Given the enormous popularity of portable music, it is not difficult to see how an idea like the iPod and iTunes would surface as something worth discussing. But the more fascinating possibility is to consider the almost endless possible new applications that PC companies could come up with, which could then become new revenue pillars. Portable computing provided by Blackberry and other similar devices is a well-known example, but there are hundreds more just lurking around the corner. In each case, the opportunity for innovation probably lies in recognizing two important principles:

- The innovation must create a use that reflects a latent or expressed consumer need that is not currently being met.
- The innovation is likely to arise from a convergence of two industries.

The beauty of this is that one immediately begins to see the vast potential for innovation even in relatively staid old industries. For example, what new opportunities might open up from the convergence of entertainment and education, including higher (university) education? Can a refrigerator that dispenses beer and has built-in television and music capabilities become the focal point of a home entertainment system? Can a car serve a purpose even when it is not being driven? What can you do with a watch besides just tell time? Can a bank be more than just a place to borrow and deposit money? Can a business school be more than just a place to get a business degree and a job? In other words, leave innovation of how your product is used by the customer to the customer and you pass up an endless stream of opportunities to grow profitably by inventing new uses for the product technologies and knowledge you already have. Think creatively about *new* uses the customer could put your product to and you open the door to unprecedented growth.

5. Putting the Framework into Practice

While the idea of dropping assumptions is simple, the difficulty lies in the subtlety. Often, we are not even aware of the assumptions we make. People have a tendency to accept something as given more as a subconscious reflex, rather than a deliberate act of compliance. Therefore, the framework we suggest requires thought and deliberation. Brainstorming practices such as those used and popularized by IDEO can be helpful in surfacing deep assumptions implicit in the way a particular product or service may be perceived. Remember: it is not about simply discarding any assumption; rather, it is about identifying and discarding the right assumption.

Our unblocking principle, as exhibited in each of the three case examples presented, can manifest itself in different ways. However, we extract some general principles of innovation, which we observe in each of the cases discussed above, as well as in other contexts. The four points below summarize what we feel are the more robust, and useful, generalizations of this principle:

- First, think of discarding assumptions that, once out of the way, allows for a *convergence* of two or more industries, such as the coffee and restaurant businesses in the case of Starbucks, and music and computers in the case of Apple. This is useful in that it can guide you to an application that is unique and more difficult to copy, hence leading towards sustainable advantage.
- Second, drop an assumption that is central to the existing paradigm, such as "coffee is a commodity and the customer cares only about price" or "aerofoil principles apply only to wings."
- Third, examine dropping an assumption that leads to an innovation that meets a latent or expressed consumer need that is currently not being met. For example, one aspect of Apple's iTunes was to allow consumers to purchase individual songs (as opposed to the Napster model) for a reasonable fee. This enabled an economical method of music distribution with broad industry support and a commercially viable business model.
- Fourth, once the initial big assumption is dropped, look for secondary assumptions that can be dropped to "refine" the innovation.

6. Conclusion

The key to innovation is creativity and the key to creativity is to think freely, without the impediment of the things we take as granted. The unblocking principle is a key element that can help both the individual and the organization to improve the quantity and quality of innovation they produce. By selectively challenging and discarding assumptions, both implicit and explicit, that dominate current thinking and application, firms can innovate free of the shackles that constrain their competitors. We provide only a sampling of the abundant list of examples of how this principle can be applied. Using the unblocking principle as often as possible, both individually and institutionally, will accelerate your organization's innovation output.

Chapter 7

Contracting for Innovation

Nick Argyres

Olin Business School,
Washington University in St. Louis

In order to compete successfully, companies are finding that it is increasingly important to capitalize on innovations generated outside the organization. Creating and capturing value from outside innovations is often difficult, however, because it involves the challenge of managing potentially hazardous contractual relationships with outside organizations, whether they be universities, firms, research institutes, etc. In this chapter, I discuss three approaches to managing these relationships: contract design, relational governance and tournaments. I discuss the relative importance of these three approaches, interactions between them, and situations in which they might substitute for, or complement, one another.

1. Introduction

For many decades, it was thought that innovation was a dish best cooked at home; companies were reluctant to seek out innovations generated outside of their organizational boundaries. There were many reasons for this. For most of the 20th century, advanced economies were less competitive than they are now. There were therefore fewer outside sources of innovation available to tap. There were fewer small firms selling technology and innovative solutions, for example, and universities were less interested in transferring their innovations to the private sector. Less developed countries produced little innovation.

Another set of reasons for companies' reluctance to embrace outside innovations is rooted in organizational inertia. Large companies with comfortable market positions often had little incentive to innovate at all, much less seek out the innovations of others. Managers developing innovations inside the company often saw outside innovations as threats to their own careers. Psychological biases against others' innovations produced the proverbial "Not Invented Here" syndrome.

Much of that has changed. Innovation now flows from a universe of companies and institutions throughout the world. Faced with more vigorous competition, companies have stronger incentives to tap into these sources though partnerships, acquisitions, special agreements, and other means. Henry Chesbrough (2005, 2006) has described this new business landscape on what he calls "open innovation."

Capitalizing on innovations from outside the organization can be quite difficult, however, even after a company has identified the outside innovations it would like to pursue. Creating and capturing value from outside innovations often involves contractual relationships with outside organizations, whether they be universities, firms, research institutes, etc. In this chapter, I discuss some of the important challenges in contracting for innovation, and describe some of the approaches companies take to address them effectively. I focus particularly on contracting scenarios in which a supplier is engaged to provide an innovative product or service to the buyer. So I have in mind contracts for R&D, product development, specialized engineering or information technology services, and the like. Such contracts are common in sectors such as aerospace, electronics, chemicals, pharmaceuticals, consumer products, transportation, etc.

2. Contracting Hazards

A fundamental challenge in contracting for innovation stems from Nobel Laureate Kenneth Arrow's "Information Paradox": Buyers are unwilling to pay for a new idea unless they have heard it first (Arrow, 1971). But once a supplier has communicated her idea to a buyer, the buyer remains unwilling to pay since he has now received the good. Of course, most nations have patent systems that aim to resolve this paradox. By first obtaining patent protection for her idea, the supplier gains legal recourse should a buyer "take the idea and run."

Patent protection, however, is often highly imperfect, and patent systems are often ineffective. When innovators are working in a "crowded" technological space, often they can secure only narrow rights to their innovation. Narrow patents are those that are easy for imitators to "invent around." Obtaining strong patent protection is particularly difficult for technologies that rely on multiple components, such as those in electronics, computer software, and telecommunications. Of course, it is often the case that an economically valuable innovation is not novel enough to earn any patent protection at all.

Even if an innovator can win a broad patent on her innovation, in some countries it is difficult and costly to enforce those rights. Developing country governments, for example, often refuse to enforce patents held by foreign companies if the imitators are domestic firms. The reason, of course, is that these governments wish to quickly stimulate economic growth in their own countries, with less concern for the longer term effects of such policies. Even in developed countries, it can be difficult to enforce patents because legal costs can be high.

A second type of hazard that can arise in contracting for innovation is what Nobel Laureate Oliver Williamson (1985) calls "asset specificity". An innovation contains asset specificity if it is custom-tailored to one particular buyer, so that its value to other buyers is much lower. The contracting hazard caused by asset specificity is that once the investment to develop the asset-specific innovation has been sunk, the buyer has an incentive to re-negotiate the deal to win better terms, knowing that the supplier's outside options are limited.

A third category of contractual hazards is uncertainty. Uncertainty can stem from many sources, but regardless of the source, it complicates the contracting process. One source of uncertainty is the nature of the contractual partner with whom a buyer or supplier is dealing. If a firm does not have a long track record of business dealings, or otherwise lacks a strong reputation for integrity, buyers or suppliers may shy away from contracting with that firm, or demand terms that are uneconomical for it. Uncertainty about the enforceability of patents or the effectiveness of the legal system can also chill efforts to contract for innovation. Contracting for innovation also typically involves technological uncertainty — uncertainty about the feasibility of innovation projects, about how technology will change during the course of the project, and about the precise nature of the buyer's needs.

In view of all these hazards of contracting for innovation, it is not surprising that for so many decades managers believed that innovation is a dish best cooked at home. Internal innovation is of course also fraught with technological uncertainty. But the hazards of dealing with a partner at arm's length, without the benefit of a hierarchical structure (i.e., a CEO) to prevent and resolve disputes that might arise, are arguably much greater than simply innovating internally.

Focusing exclusively on internal innovation, however, is no longer feasible for many industrial companies. Firms now compete fiercely to gain access to sources of innovation wherever they may be located. Companies that fail to find ways to mitigate the hazards of contracting for innovation will fall prey to rivals who *have* cracked this nut.

3. Contract Design

So how do companies crack the nut? How do they mitigate the hazards in contracting for innovation? In the remainder of this chapter, I discuss three approaches to hazard mitigation, none of which are mutually exclusive: contract design, relational governance, and tournaments.

A fundamental assumption made by most economists who study contracts is that contracts are unavoidably incomplete. By "incomplete" they mean that contracts inevitably leave out contingencies that the parties did not or could not anticipate beforehand, so that were that contingency to actually occur and a dispute about it arise, a court or arbiter would not know how to rule.

An example of an incomplete contract might be a contract that specifies some but not all of the desired performance features of the product or service to be delivered. For example, a buyer might contract for a piece of custom software that turns out to be of poor quality because, while it works well on the supplier's computers, it fails on the buyer's computer due to interferences with other software on the buyer's computer that would have been difficult to anticipate beforehand.

Economists have argued that if parties to a contract *could* anticipate all possible contingencies and describe them unambiguously, all contractual hazards could be handled in contracts. In this kind of world, all economic activity could occur through contracts, leaving no reason to have large hierarchical firms that guide economic activity using what Alfred Chandler called "the visible hand" of administrative directive (Chandler, 1977). This idea forms the basis for Oliver Williamson's Nobel Prize-winning research, as well as for influential work by Oliver Hart, Sanford Grossman and John Moore (Grossman and Hart, 1986; Hart and Moore, 1990).

While this idea is indeed a fundamental insight, it does not address the important reality that contracts differ in their *degree of completeness*. It tells us that all contracts are incomplete and that is why hazardous exchanges are managed within firms, but why are some contracts more complete than others? More importantly, for managers facing the imperative to contract for innovation, can contracts be made more complete in order to mitigate the hazards of contracting for innovation?

We actually know very little about *how* incomplete contracts are, why they are as incomplete as they are, and whether highly incomplete contracts are for some reason optimal for some kinds of exchanges. Some progress has been made, however. In a study of high-technology defense contracts, Keith Crocker and Scott Reynolds found that projects featuring greater technological uncertainty tended to be managed under more incomplete contracts, using cost-plus contracting, whereas projects with less such uncertainty were governed by more complete contracts using fixed price or cost-plus-incentive-fee arrangements (Crocker and Reynolds, 1993). This result is not terribly surprising, but it does show that the nature of the project can have an impact on the incompleteness of the contract. It therefore suggests that contracting partners invest less in contract development when technological uncertainty is so high that foreseeing many contingencies is extremely difficult.

A second study offers some theoretical reasons for why contracting parties might decide not to develop more complete contracts even if they could. Douglas Bernheim and Michael Whinston developed a model of a contractual relationship with mutual obligations (Bernheim and Whinston, 1998). They showed that if performance by Party A is less measurable than performance by Party B, further specifying B's obligations would put Party A at a disadvantage if the parties were to end up in court. This is because Party B would have an easier time demonstrating that he fulfilled his obligations than Party A would. Party A therefore prefers a more incomplete contract, and will get its way as long as it has a bit of bargaining power.

For example, an employment contract between a school and a teacher may be left deliberately vague regarding the teacher's specific responsibilities. The reason is that while it is often easy for courts to identify whether the school has fulfilled its obligation to the teacher, some aspects of teacher performance are difficult to measure. This makes it difficult to judge whether a teacher has fulfilled his/her obligations under the contract.

The Bernheim and Whinston model is intriguing. However, it has not been tested empirically, and it suffers from at least two drawbacks as a general explanation for contract incompleteness. First, in many contracts for innovation, the major obligations lie on the supplier's side. The buyer may have obligations too, but they are not significant enough to create the kinds of problems in the model. Second, contracting for innovation often involves multiple highly technical, hard-to-measure tasks, so much so that courts could not adjudicate them efficiently were they to come into dispute. In these cases, the parties are not able to anticipate a court's responses to different contract designs. Indeed, in a recent study of high-technology contracts in telecommunications industries, Michael Ryall and Rachelle Sampson (2009) found that firms developed and relied on contracts that they knew were unenforceable in court. This finding is a bit of a puzzle in itself, but also points to some limitations of the Bernheim and Whinston theory.

An arguably more powerful explanation for why contracts for innovation are incomplete has been developed in recent work on the topic of "learning to contract." The very definition of contracting for innovation implies contracting for something new; something that has not been previously contracted for in exactly the same way. For these transactions, standard form, boilerplate-type contracts are of limited use. Major sections of the contract must be custom-designed to the transaction. In many cases of contracting for innovation, it is not obvious to the parties how this should be done.

In recent work with Kyle Mayer, I described a case in which two firms in an emerging industry (personal computers in the 1980s) required several years before arriving at a contractual structure that adequately addressed the contractual hazards discussed above (Mayer and Argyres,

2004). This occurred largely because it took a long time for the parties to understand what the hazards were in their particular context, and how to address them with appropriate contractual provisions. Moreover, the firms seemed to make different kinds of mistakes in contract design that they only recognized after the fact. Follow-on work with Mayer and Janet Bercovitz shows evidence of learning to contract over time in a larger sample of contracts from information technology services (Argyres, Bercovitz and Mayer, 2007).

This research on learning to contract suggests, then, that contract design can be an important way in which firms safeguard transactions for innovation, but firms may need time and resources to learn how to design contracts adequately. This is especially the case in new industries, or when the innovations under contract are quite novel. Firms in more established industries contracting for less novel innovations — product or service upgrades, for example — are less likely to face a steep learning curve for contract design. For these firms, contract design will be more straightforward.

The next logical question for managers interested in contracting for highly novel innovation is, "How can we speed up the process of learning to contract?" This is a question that has barely been addressed in management research. In my work with Mayer, we suggest that firms can use their own past contracts as a repository of knowledge of best and worst contracting practices. Managers can study these contracts with those who developed them in order to glean insights into problematic areas. Often, for example, firms tend to focus on issues like payment terms, protection of property rights to the innovation and the like, all of which are of course very important. There is often less attention paid, however, to matters such as how the two parties are to communicate with each other as events unfold during contract execution. Disputes sometimes arise not because parties' needs have changed in ways that are fundamentally irreconcilable, but because the contract did not adequately specify how and when communication of those changes in needs is to occur. Contracts can thus be viewed not only as documents for protecting the parties' interests and investments, but also as guides for how the two parties will work together over the course of the project. In that sense, contracts are as much managerial tools as they are legal safeguards. Indeed, this view of contracts helps explain the puzzle mentioned earlier about why firms sometimes design legally unenforceable contracts. Even if unenforceable, the process of designing contracts may help the parties to better understand the hazards and challenges of managing the kind of transaction they desire.

This emphasis on the managerial functions of contracts (as opposed to the legal functions only) immediately implies that speeding up the process of learning to contract requires the active participation of managers and engineers in contract design. Many managers, and perhaps more engineers, are reluctant to spend much time on contract design. Both groups often have other pressing priorities. Engineers are often pushing to meet product development deadlines. Managers are busy "putting out fires" and do not feel they have the luxury of planning exchanges and imagining contingencies that may or may not occur in the future. "Leave it to the lawyers," they think.

However, it is difficult to imagine most contract lawyers writing the following key clause from a software development contract: "BIOS modifications will include: creating a devnode for the controller; describing the controller to the PCI BIOS (bus number, device number, IRQ mapping); routing of a PCI IRQ to the controller during POST ... The programmable I/O ranges of the [supplier chip designation] chipset will be configured to support the custom gate array."

My work with Kyle Mayer suggests that inadequate participation by managers and engineers in the contract design process jeopardizes the effectiveness of contracting for innovation (Argyres and Mayer, 2007). That participation is sorely needed to develop the task descriptions, contingency plans, and communication protocols that are so central to high-performance contracting. Lawyers of course also play important roles in contract design, but their expertise usually lies in different areas, such as design of rights to intellectual property developed in the relationship and design of dispute resolution procedures. Developing effective contract designs thus involves ensuring the participation of managers and engineers, and allocating tasks to designers to take advantage of specialization of knowledge.

Contract design, then, is an important way in which companies seek to protect themselves from the various kinds of hazards that could arise when contracting for innovation. The process of designing contracts, however, can also stimulate processes in which managers learn about the exchanges they are engaging in, which is important when those exchanges involve a significant amount of novel activity. Contracts should therefore be seen not only as providing safeguards, but more broadly as providing a framework for planning collaborative innovation effort.

4. Relational Governance

A thoughtful contract design is of course no guarantee that things will go smoothly. Divisive contingencies that the parties could not have anticipated, or only could have anticipated with great investment, can always arise. Such events pose few serious problems if the parties are not dependent upon each other, but in most cases of contracting for innovation, dependency is a given.

Companies therefore sometimes seek to support their contractual design efforts by developing long-term relationships with their partners. The idea is to foster a relationship of mutual trust, so that if contingencies not addressed in the contract do arise, the parties can still "work things out" based on their trust in each other's desire to continue the relationship into the future. The hope is that this "shadow of the future" will cement the relationship as it experiences "the slings and arrows of fortune." This approach to managing inter-firm exchanges is called "relational governance."

There is great controversy among organizational scholars about just how important the role of relational governance is in contracting for innovation. On one extreme are sociology-oriented scholars who argue that because of the uncertainty in these kinds of exchanges, trust is indispensible. They argue that there is often enough trust such that detailed contracts are, or at least become, unimportant. Indeed, contracts can even be detrimental in this view; they destroy trust by transforming the exchange from relational to "transactional." If the parties treat an exchange as merely transactional, they are more likely to try to take advantage of their partner if the opportunity arises. In this way, the thinking goes, detailed contracts end up producing the behavior they are designed to prevent.

On the other extreme are economics-oriented scholars who believe that trust plays a minor role in most commercial transactions. In their view, companies are hard-nosed, sophisticated entities that understand that their contractual partners are not altruistic charities, but are in business to make money. To the extent that companies occasionally transact for products or services without detailed contracts, they do so based on the calculation that the partner's concern for its reputation in the market will deter it from taking advantage of unanticipated contingencies. Oliver Williamson, for example, argued that if "trust" comes down to "trust in a reputation", then one might as well speak of reputation and not a murky concept like "trust" (Williamson, 1996).

Between these two extremes are those who see companies as mostly sophisticated and forward-looking, but also as managed by human beings whose decisions are often influenced by emotions. With this perspective, neither blind trust nor contracts alone are sufficient to cement exchange relationships in the uncertain environments in which companies contract for innovation. On one hand, an overemphasis on contractual detail without attention to the development of trust can poison the atmosphere in a relationship. On the other hand, relying solely on efforts to develop trust leaves one or both parties unduly exposed. Companies are reluctant to leave themselves so vulnerable, and if they do, they are likely to get burned sooner or later.

This middle-of-the-road perspective implies that in most contracting situations, companies ought to invest in developing detailed contractual designs while also fostering trust with the partner. Striking this balance involves placing heavy emphasis on those aspects of the contracts that involve communication between the parties and contingency planning. Protections and safeguards are not ignored in the contract design, but are not treated as more important than the provisions aimed at outlining the framework for collaboration.

For example, in the software development contracts that I studied with Kyle Mayer, repeated communication problems led one of the parties to add a section entitled "Project Reporting and Performance" to its contract template. This section clarified exactly how often Compustar was required to update the customer with different types of information (e.g., technical problems, schedule issues, external concerns). The section also included the requirements for any milestones in the contract.

Strategy researchers have produced evidence supporting both the trust-based view and the middle-of-the-road view. Much of the research supporting the trust-based view is problematic, however, because trust is often not carefully and consistently defined within and across the studies (as distinct from reputation, for example), because studies often measure trust using naïve survey questions, and alternative mechanisms that may be in place (such as contracts) are often unaccounted for. Another problem is that most of the studies address relationships in which trust is already present (or not), rather than how trust is developed. There are, however, a few studies of the latter, and some carefully conducted experimental studies suggesting that an emphasis on contracts can drive out trust.

There is also evidence, however, that relational governance and detailed contracts reinforce each other rather than operate at cross-purposes. A few empirical studies suggest that the contract design process, if focused sufficiently on establishing communication protocols and outlining the roles and responsibilities of the parties, can actually enhance trust rather than detract from it. They suggest that contracts may be necessary before trust has developed, and that over time, they are used increasingly as a framework for managing the exchange, as concerns for safeguarding assets diminish somewhat. The issue is by no means settled, however. More research is needed into when relational governance and contracting are substitutes for each other, and when they are complementary.

5. Tournaments

The third approach I will discuss for contracting for innovation is what I will label "tournaments". By "tournaments" I have in mind arrangements in which a buyer of innovative products or services ensures supplier performance not so much by detailed contracts or relational governance, but by structuring competition between suppliers over time. This approach is used when the buyer requires a flow of innovative products or services from a supplier over time; where the transaction involves more than a one-time delivery.

In this approach, the buyer relies heavily on the promise of future business to motivate the supplier to innovate. The approach is often used in conjunction with contracts and/or relational contracting, but the heavy lifting is done by the "tournament" structure of the arrangements. With tournaments, contracts can be less detailed than otherwise, and trust need not run as deep.

Tournaments typically involve the buyer establishing a hierarchy of suppliers, in which the higher tiers enjoy more profitable contracts from the buyer, and/or stronger guarantees of future business, with the lower tiers featuring lower-profit contracts and no guarantees of future business. Suppliers starting at lower tiers have the opportunity to move to higher tiers should they innovate in ways that the buyer deems valuable. Those that fail move down the hierarchy, or out completely.

To make this kind of system work, the buyer must invest heavily in systems for monitoring supplier performance. The buyer must usually invest not only in inspecting and measuring supplier outputs, but in inspecting and measuring supplier processes. Only with careful measurement can the buyer reliably compare the performances of different suppliers for purposes of placement in the supplier hierarchy. The buyer may also invest in helping suppliers meet the buyers' requirements for innovation by sharing technology, management know-how, and the like. Susan Helper, John Paul MacDuffie, Charles Sabel, Ronald Gilson and others have studied such tournament-like arrangements in the Japanese auto and electronics industries (Helper, MacDuffie and Sabel, 2000; Gilson, Sabel and Scott, 2009).

While Toyota, for example, has recently experienced problems with its North American and European suppliers, it has a long history of very successful relationships with its Japanese suppliers. These relationships are built on numerous elements. For example, Toyota invests heavily in training its suppliers, and in equipment used by suppliers that is specialized to Toyota. Toyota also shares proprietary information with suppliers so as to help improve their productivity. On the other hand, many suppliers invest heavily in learning the Toyota system, and in producing Toyota-specific components. These reciprocal investments help bond the relationships.

However, one of the other key elements of Toyota's system is that Toyota evaluates all of its suppliers annually, and uses that information to decide which will receive more Toyota business, and which will not. So the system has a tournament-like flavor in this respect.

An interesting aspect of tournaments arrangements is that, even with reciprocal investments, suppliers are usually more dependent on the buyer than vice versa. While the buyer may make some investments in supplier monitoring and education that cannot be reused for other suppliers, these

investments are usually a far smaller fraction of the buyer's total investments than the proportion of the supplier's total investments that are totally
dedicated to meeting the buyer's specific requirements. Suppliers at various
tiers in a tournament often sell a very high proportion of their output to the
buyer. The question is, why would a supplier be willing to enter a relationship of great dependency, when the buyer is not nearly as dependent?

One reason might be that the supplier has already made sunk
investments that cannot be re-used in other industries, and the buyer is one
of the "only games in town" in that industry. In this case, the buyer has
what economists call "monopsony power": i.e., bargaining power that
allows the buyer to set many of the terms under which it deals with
suppliers. Because suppliers have few good alternatives, they accept the
tournament system and try to make the best of it. The buyer ensures that
the supplier earns just enough profit to remain in the hierarchy (if it meets
minimum standards for innovation), but no more.

A second reason why suppliers may be willing to become dependent on
the buyer is that a culture of community solidarity and conformism in
business, and in society more broadly, provides assurance that the buyer
will not take advantage of the supplier. Japanese society is thought to have
these kinds of characteristics, for example.

These two conditions, however — monopsony power and societal-level
trust — suggest that tournament models for contracting for innovation
may be limited in the breadth of their applicability. Significant monopsony power is present in only a fraction of industries, and where it is
present, suppliers face strong incentives to redirect future investments
towards other buyers in other industries or industry segments. Similarly,
while high levels of trust may prevail in Japanese society, they are not
present in many other societies in the same way. Thus, while tournament
arrangements may be well-suited for certain specific industry settings,
they are not likely to provide a general model for contracting for
innovation.

6. Putting the Framework into Practice

The three-approach framework I outlined in this chapter contains a
number of implications for managers. First, it suggests that because

contracting for innovation is a hazardous exercise, it requires investment in contract design capabilities within the firm. These capabilities should reside in teams of managers, engineers and in-house attorneys. Second, it suggests that while relational governance may be a useful complement to enforcing contracts for innovation, it is unlikely to be a good substitute. Finally, tournaments among suppliers are an attractive way to achieve efficient contracting for innovation, but to work well they may require special conditions that are not present in most industries.

7. Conclusion

Contracting for innovation is fraught with hazards. Yet it is a competitive imperative in many industries. Indeed, as the sources of innovation continue to proliferate worldwide, a firm's competitive advantage will increasingly come to rest on its ability to mitigate these hazards. In this chapter, I discussed three approaches to hazard mitigation: contract design, relational contracting and tournaments. I suggested that contract design is perhaps the most generally applicable approach, and for that reason deserves special attention from managers. However, in some particular settings, relational contracting or tournaments may be important mechanisms as well. Still, developing a better understanding about how each of these mechanisms work, and when they effectively substitute and/or complement each other, is critical for academics and practitioners alike.

References

Argyres, Nicholas and Kyle Mayer (2007). Contract Design as a Firm Capability: An Integration of Learning and Transaction Cost Perspectives. *Academy of Management Review*, 32: 1060–1077.

Argyres, Nicholas, Janet Bercovitz and Kyle Mayer (2007). Complementarity and Evolution of Contractual Provisions: An Empirical Study of IT Services Contracts. *Organization Science*, 18: 3–19.

Arrow, Kenneth (1971). *Essays on the Theory of Risk Bearing*. Amsterdam: North Holland.

Bernheim, B. Douglas and Michael Whinston (1998). Incomplete Contracts and Strategic Ambiguity. *American Economic Review*, 88: 902–932.

Chandler, Alfred (1977). *The Visible Hand: The Managerial Revolution in American Business.* Boston, MA: Belknap Press.

Chesbrough, Henry (2005). *Open Innovation: The New Imperative for Creating and Profiting from Technology.* Boston, MA: Harvard Business School Publishing.

Chesbrough, Henry (2006). *Open Business Models: How to Thrive in the New Innovation Landscape.* Boston, MA: Harvard Business School Publishing.

Chesbrough, Henry, Wim Vanhaverbeke and Joel West (2008). *Open Innovation: Researching a New Paradigm.* New York: Oxford University Press.

Crocker, Keith and Scott Reynolds (1993). The Efficiency of Incomplete Contracts: An Empirical Analysis of Air Force Engine Procurement. *RAND Journal of Economics*, 24: 126–146.

Gilson, Ronald, Charles Sabel and Richard Scott (2009). Contracting for Innovation: Vertical Disintegration and Interfirm Collaboration. *Columbia Law Review*, 109: 431–502.

Grossman, Sanford and Oliver Hart (1986). The Costs and Benefits of Ownership: A Theory of Vertical and Lateral Integration. *Journal of Political Economy*, 94: 691–719.

Hart, Oliver and John Moore (1990). Property Rights and the Nature of the Firm. *Journal of Political Economy*, 98: 1119–1158.

Helper, Susan, John Paul MacDuffie and Charles Sabel (2000). Pragmatic Collaborations: Advancing Knowledge While Controlling Opportunism. *Industrial and Corporate Change*, 9: 443–489.

Mayer, Kyle and Nicholas Argyres (2004). Learning to Contract: Evidence from the Personal Computer Industry. *Organization Science*, 5: 394–410.

Ryall, M. and R. Sampson (2009). Formal Contracts in the Presence of Relational Enforcement Mechanisms: Evidence from Technology Development Contracts. *Management Science*, 55: 906–925.

Williamson, Oliver (1985). *The Economic Institutions of Capitalism.* New York: The Free Press.

Williamson, Oliver (1996). *The Mechanisms of Governance.* New York: Oxford University Press.

Chapter 8

R&D Mythbusters

Anne Marie Knott

Associate Professor of Strategy,
Olin Business School, Washington University in St. Louis

Industry R&D is one of the main sources of national economic growth as well as one of the main sources of value creation for firms. Accordingly it has received considerable attention from both economists and management scholars. Many of the prescriptions advanced by past theory have taken root both because they have intuitive appeal and because prior empirical data and techniques were not sophisticated enough to refute them. More recent work which combines insider experience with more sophisticated data and methods demonstrates that many of the prescriptions from past theory are invalid. These busted myths have implications for both government technology policy and firm R&D strategy.

I became an academic after an initial career in defense electronics at Hughes Aircraft Company. While nominally my job at Hughes was designing missile guidance systems, I averred that my *real* job was "pushing the knowledge frontier". Accordingly, two things pushed/pulled me toward academics from industry: (1) The government was making acquisition decisions that suppressed incentives for company investment in R&D, and (2) Hughes' acquisition by GM shifted R&D project selection methodology from a "college of cardinals" assessing the technological future to one driven by return on investment (ROI).

Thus, to my mind, both the government and the new executive office were compromising the US engine of growth. For those unfamiliar with Hughes (beyond its "notorious" founder), it was responsible for a number of very important general purpose technologies including: geosynchronous orbit (communications satellite), the laser and the now

defunct transistor. It was a great place to work. I remember once asking
a customer how he viewed Hughes relative to our competitors. He said,
"I go to you guys when I don't know what I want; once you figure that
out, I can go to the other guys to build it — because they're less expen-
sive." He was wrong about the other guys building it, but that's another
story.

The point is, I became an academic because it seemed neither the government (at the industrial policy level) nor the company (at the firm level)
knew what was important for sustainable innovation. Moreover, since the
government had RAND and a myriad of other economists at its disposal,
the economists must not understand either.

So I was and wasn't surprised to learn early in my studies that Industrial
Organization economics prescribed concentrated industries (muted competition) as the optimal market structure for innovation. The surprise was
that academics didn't match prevailing wisdom from practice: Most engineers believe that competition stimulates innovation. Indeed, some firms
carry parallel projects for new technologies to stimulate in-house competition. The lack of surprise was that something in the literature had to
explain why government policies were inconsistent with practical
intuition.

My academic career then has been one of digging wide and deep into
the literature to understand current thought on the optimal environment
for innovation. When theory/empirics didn't match intuition from industry, I tried to understand the disconnect. Thus, I view my career to date
as one of "R&D mythbusting". That of course wasn't my intent, but
rather a byproduct of search for the "true model" of the R&D growth
engine. This chapter summarizes eight myths, the puzzles they pose, and
the revealed truth from recent empirical studies that resolves the
puzzles.

Myth 1: Asset Mass Efficiency

Asset Mass Efficiency was an argument advanced in a 1989 paper by
Ingemar Dierickx and Karel Cool, in an interesting model of knowledge
accumulation. The basic idea of asset mass efficiency is that the stock of

knowledge (accumulated R&D spending) enhances the productivity of current R&D spending:

> *"Sustainability will be enhanced to the extent that adding increments to an existing asset stock is facilitated by possessing high levels of that stock. The underlying notion is that 'success breeds success': historical success translates into favorable initial asset stock positions which in turn facilitate further asset accumulation."*
>
> — Dierickx and Cool (1989)

The puzzle — If this were true, then entrants couldn't catch up to leaders, and the most innovative firms in an industry would be the oldest firms. While this is true in some cases, the prevailing perception is that the most innovative firms are start-ups and that old firms stifle creativity. On average, small firms are at least as productive (if not more productive) with their R&D spending than large firms.

The revealed truth — There are no asset mass efficiencies. Rather, depreciation/obsolescence rates are so high in most industries that entrants could catch up to the knowledge stock of leaders if they matched leader spending for three years (see Figure 1). Of course, they have trouble doing that because they don't have the same financial resources.

Implication — Incumbent firms have to work very hard merely to maintain existing knowledge stocks. This is sometimes known as the Red Queen effect.

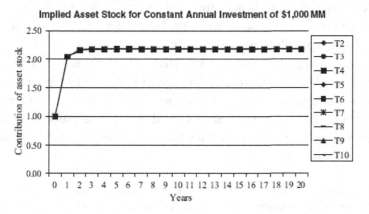

Figure 1.

Myth 2: Absorptive Capacity

Absorptive capacity is an argument very similar to asset mass efficiency. It was advanced by Dan Levinthal and Wes Cohen in two articles in 1989/1990. Just as Dierickx and Cool argue that past R&D spending affects the productivity of current R&D spending, Cohen and Levinthal argue that past R&D spending enhances firms' ability to utilize spillovers[1] from the R&D of others. Thus, returns to spillovers increase with the firm's own R&D spending:

> *"We argue that the ability to evaluate and utilize outside knowledge is largely a function of the level of prior related knowledge. At the most elemental level, this prior knowledge includes basic skills or even a shared language but may also include knowledge of the most recent scientific or technological developments in a given field. Thus, prior related knowledge confers an ability to recognize the value of new information, assimilate it, and apply it to commercial ends. These abilities collectively constitute what we call a firm's 'absorptive capacity.'"*
>
> — Cohen and Levinthal (1990)

The absorptive capacity argument appeared plausible because there is a positive relationship between R&D investment and the rate of return on those investments (Figure 2). There was no alternative explanation for this in the literature.

The puzzle — Firms who have done the greatest amount of R&D are the ones least likely to benefit from spillovers. They typically are at the knowledge frontier, and accordingly the knowledge held by rivals is likely to be redundant with what they already know.

The revealed truth — Firms, like individuals, differ in their IQ (ability to solve problems they haven't encountered before). For any given level of R&D, the high IQ firm has greater innovative output. Thus, their optimal level of R&D is greater. So it's not that larger investments generate higher returns (from spillovers), it's that higher returns create incentives

---

[1] Spillovers are the leakage of knowledge between firms. They can occur overtly from imitation/reverse engineering or passively through personnel movement, industry conferences and transactions with buyers and suppliers.

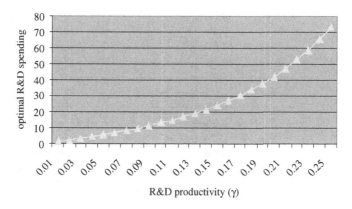

Figure 2.

for greater investment. Moreover, IQ is *inversely* related to firms' ability to make use of spillovers — those spending more (because of high IQ) make poor use of spillovers. As an example, the IQ of Intel is estimated to be 124, while that of AMD is estimated to be 114. The spillover elasticity for both firms is 0, meaning they derive no benefit from spillovers.

Implication — Innovative firms can probably abandon efforts to gain knowledge from rivals (other than for competitive rationale). Conversely, imitative firms (those with low IQ, but high absorptive capacity) should develop capability to make better use of spillovers. Additionally, they can probably reduce investment in innovative R&D.

Myth 3: Spillovers/Imitation Inhibits Innovation

The advantage of spillovers for laggards and the economy is obvious. They help reduce a firm's cost to achieve a given level of technology. A long-held view in Industrial Organization economics is that spillovers are a dual-edged sword because knowing innovations will be imitated reduces incentives to innovate.

The puzzle — While in principle anticipating imitation could reduce entry into new markets, new firms enter industry each year at a rate of about 10% of established firms.

The revealed truth — In a study of the 25 leading R&D industries, innovation is highest in industries with the highest spillover rates. Each

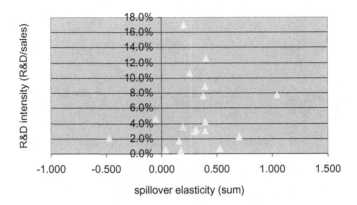

Figure 3.   R&D spending versus spillovers

10% increase in spillover elasticity[2] is associated with a 4.2% increase in R&D spending (Figure 3). Thus, it appears that spillovers actually *stimulate* innovation. Rather than looking forward at what might happen if they imitate, firms seem to be looking backward at what happens after they are imitated. Once they are imitated, they lose profits and face a choice of exiting the market or innovating again. In general they choose to innovate again to regain lost profits.

Implication — At the policy level: because firms are backward-looking, patents probably have minimal impact on the level of innovation. In fact, Merck is now moving toward trade secrets rather than patents to protect its new drugs. At the firm level: firms should develop other mechanisms to ensure they capture the necessary returns to innovation before imitation. The best mechanisms appear to be a strong brand, strong marketing, or large-scale distribution/manufacturing.

Myth 4: Concentrated Industries are Optimal for Innovation

A related prescription in Industrial Organization derives from the belief that spillovers inhibit innovation. It is the prescription that concentrated industries are the optimal market structure for innovation. Monopolists have little incentive to innovate because innovations cannibalize existing

---

[2]The productivity of rival spillovers with respect to one's own output.

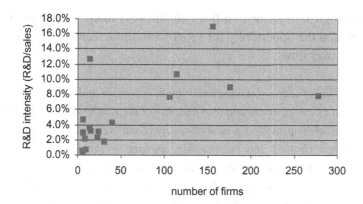

Figure 4. R&D spending versus industry concentration

profits. At the other extreme, highly competitive industries increase the probability of imitation and thus also reduce the returns to innovation.

The puzzle — The electronics industry (particularly as incarnated in Silicon Valley) is simultaneously one of the most competitive industries.

The revealed truth — Innovation increases with competition (the number of firms) (Figure 4). Michael Porter has probably done the best job of demonstrating this via the qualitative study in his 1990 book, *The Competitive Advantage of Nations.* He studied 500 national industries to understand what local factors led to global advantage — intense local rivalry was one of the most significant factors. (Note this prescription is particularly delightful coming from the insulated industry guy of *Competitive Strategy.*) Complementing Porter's case studies is a large numbers study in banking that inherently controls for everything other than market structure. That study found not only that innovation increases with the number of competitors, but that competitive pressure from lagging firms (those with higher costs) is three times that for leading firms. This reinforces the idea that imitation eating away profits (rather than a race to secure a monopoly) is the real stimulus to innovation.

Myth 5: Technological Opportunity Becomes Exhausted

In 1986, Richard Foster introduced his idea of a technological "S-curve." The basic idea (adopted from prior academic work) by Nelson and Winter on technological trajectories is that industries are linked to particular technologies, and the opportunity for progress in these technologies becomes exhausted over time:

> "The beliefs of successful companies are based on an understanding of the dynamics of competition, and in particular of the relationship between the effort put into improving a product or process and the results achieved over time. When charted, this relationship appears as the familiar S-curve. Initially, as funds are put into developing a new product or process, progress is very slow. Then, as the key knowledge necessary to make advances is put in place, the pace of progress surges. Finally, as more dollars are put into the development of a product or process, it becomes more and more difficult and expensive to make technical progress."
>
> — Foster (1986)

The puzzle — Probably the most compelling counter-example to technological limits is agriculture. This is undoubtedly the oldest economic sector to employ technology (war and construction being the obvious contenders). Agriculture has consistently shown dramatic improvement in yield per acre (Figure 5).

The revealed truth — On average, technological opportunity in an industry tends to increase over time. In a study of 25 R&D-intensive industries over the period 1980–2000, technological opportunity (the returns to R&D investment) was decreasing in only three industries: petroleum, plastic resin and electrical equipment.

Implication — Firms in innovative industries (which we now know to be ones with high spillovers and vigorous rivalry) seem able to renew technological opportunity. Thus, firms in those industries must make the investments necessary to keep pace with the moving frontier (Figure 6).

Myth 6: As Industries Age, It is Easier to Exploit Spillovers

In a 2002 article, Lynne Zucker, Michael Darby and Jeff Armstrong suggested that industries follow a spillover life cycle where initially only core researchers can enter a new industry. Thereafter, the science/technology

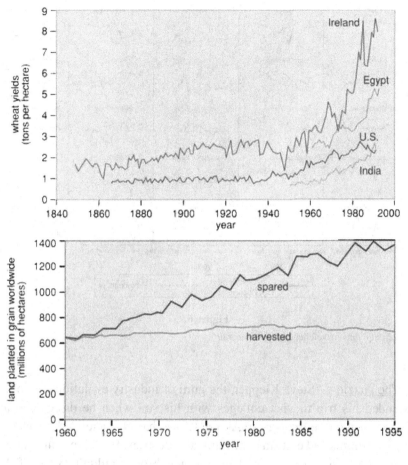

Figure 5.

becomes incorporated in coursework/books to train/attract future employees, so industry knowledge diffuses more rapidly:

> *"We believe that, at least for the first 10 or 15 years, the innovations which underlie biotechnology are properly analyzed in terms of naturally excludable knowledge held by a small initial group of discoverers, their coworkers, and others who learned the knowledge from working at the bench-science level with those possessing the requisite know-how. Ultimately the knowledge spread sufficiently widely to become part of routine science which could be learned at any major research university."*
>
> — Zucker, Darby and Armstrong (2002)

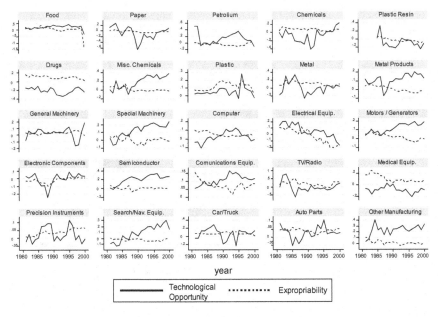

Figure 6.

Source: http://phe.rockefeller.edu/sparetheearth/

The puzzle — Steve Klepper, the guru of industry evolutions (he once extended his trip to visit colleges with his son when he discovered an archive of the tyre industry in Akron, Ohio), has characterized the evolution of entrants and exits in concentrated industries. In all those industries, entry decreases after an initial period, which we wouldn't expect if the requisite knowledge became more accessible over time.

The revealed truth — On average, spillover elasticity decreases over time. The same study that characterized technological opportunity for 25 industries over time also characterized spillover elasticity. Spillover elasticity increases over time in only one industry, precision instruments. In all other industries, it decreases or remains constant.

Implication — It appears the two trends (increasing technological opportunity and decreasing spillover elasticity) may be related. As industries age, firms become better at moving the technological frontier, and this movement becomes increasingly difficult for imitators to track.

Myth 7: Smart Managers Get Blindsided by New Technology

A number of classic studies explain the death of former industry leaders on managers' cognitive biases precluding them from seeing the future. These include buddy whip, photolithography, large steel and disk drive manufacturers.

The puzzle — Most CEOs (particularly those who rose through the company ranks by outperforming all their peers) are pretty smart, and make it their business to know future competition and technology.

The revealed truth — Monopoly/oligopoly positions distort incentives. In every case (USX, Photolithography, Kodak, Disk drives) for which data is available, the incumbents had near monopoly positions and vintage capital. Thus, at every point they compared the net present value of current technology/market versus pursuing the new technology/market, the net present value (NPV) of the current technology/market was higher.

Implication — Avoid the soft life. While concentrated industries offer higher accounting profits, they present the risk of obsolescence (where the accounting profits ultimately cease). Better still, while concentrated industries offer higher accounting profits than competitive industries, a study by Robinson and Hou shows that competitive industries offer higher stock market returns.

Myth 8: Spillovers are Like Air — Everyone Benefits Equally

Industrial Organization models of competitive R&D treat spillovers as a pool of knowledge which has equal value to all rivals in the industry. Thus, Intel and AMD benefit equally from each other's R&D.

The puzzle — The wedge mentioned for absorptive capacity is even more applicable here; it's unlikely that the Intel who spends 32% of industry R&D has anything to learn from the numerous semiconductor firms who conduct less R&D, including AMD who spends 5% of industry R&D.

The revealed truth — Firms differ both in the size of their relevant spillover pool (only knowledge held by superior firms contributes to innovative output) and in their ability to use the pool to generate innovative output (spillover elasticity). In the IQ study, the firms who benefit most from spillovers are the laggard firms with low IQs. They have large spillover pools and are more effective at using the spillovers to generate innovative output.

Implication — Firms with low innovative IQ seem to have an offsetting advantage: high imitative IQ. This fundamental difference of firms seems to explain the source for the classic dichotomy between innovators and imitators.

Conclusion

In this chapter I have stated eight important beliefs about innovation and exposed these as myths, based on logic and fact.

If all these myths were merely scattered bits of wisdom, mythbusting would have been an exercise in frustration. But there is a pattern to these myths. They all pertain to a worldview where innovation advantage is wrested with large, insulated firms. Incidentally, this is precisely the prescription reached by Schumpeter (our hero of creative destruction). In his later work he propounded the view that large, monopolistic enterprises were the appropriate engine for economic growth.

What the mythbusting exercise has shown is that Schumpeter is at least partially wrong. The large firm may still be the engine of economic growth (77.3% of US R&D is performed by the 3.9% of firms with more than 1,000 employees), but this is only true when there are other firms riding its draft and eroding its profits. This parallax view of the world is captured informally in the cases from Porter's *Competitive Advantage of Nations*, and captured more formally in work by Aghion, Harris, Howitt, and Vickers.

In this new world, the large firm is a Red Queen who is working hard merely to maintain her relative market share. But she is heroic — she drives the innovation engine that is responsible for the vast majority of economic growth. Better still, she is not a martyr in this. While she may envy the soft life and higher profitability of her more monopolistic peers, she accrues higher stock market returns than her complacent counterparts. Embrace the new reality.

References

Cohen, Wesley M. and Levinthal, Daniel A. (1990). Absorptive Capacity: A New Perspective on Learning and Innovation. *Administrative Science Quarterly*, 35(1): 128–152.

Dierickx, Ingemar and Cool, Karel (1989). Asset Stock Accumulation and Sustainability of Competitive Advantage. *Management Science*, 35(12): 1504–1511.

Foster, Richard N. (1986). Attacking through Innovation. *McKinsey Quarterly*, (3): 2–12.

Zucker, Lynne G., Darby, Michael R. and Armstrong, Jeff S. (2002). Commercializing Knowledge: University Science, Knowledge Capture, and Firm Performance in Biotechnology. *Management Science*, 48(1): 138–153.

Index